The Wonder Is

The Wonder Is

New and Selected Poems
1974-2012

Jan Seale

Revised, expanded edition, Ink Brush Press, 2012
First edition: Panther Creek Press, 2005

Cover Design: Erren Seale

ISBN: 978-0-9835968-9-9
Library of Congress Control Number: 2012931104

Manufactured in the United States

Ink Brush Press
Temple and Dallas, Texas

Acknowledgements

For the encouragement of first publication of various poems in this volume, the poet acknowledges with gratitude the following:

Periodicals

Aileron, Alacrán, Ancient Cud, Art E, Artword Quarterly, Austin Writer, Blue Mesa Review, Calyx, The Cape Rock, CCTE Proceedings, Concho River Review, Crab Creek Review, descant, Encodings, Grasslands Review, Gray Sky Review, Hodge Podge Poetry, Iron Horse Literary Review, Isosceles, Journal of English-Teaching Techniques, Kalliope, Latitude 30° 18', Mediphors, Mesquite Review, Midwest Poetry Review, Nebo, New America, New Mexico Humanities Review, Nimrod, Phoebe, Pikestaff Forum, Plumbline, Right Hand Pointing, riverSedge, Rockhurst Review, Rocky Mt. Review of Language and Literature, Right Hand Pointing, Small Pond, South Florida Poetry Review, Southwestern American Literature, The Student, Sulphur River Poetry Review, ¡Tex!, Texas College English, The Texas Observer, The Texas Review, Vanderbilt Street Review, Visions, Wind Literary Journal

Anthologies

Cries of the Spirit (Beacon Press), *For She Is the Tree of Life* (Conari Press), *Great Plains Poetry Anthology* (Point Riders Press), *Mixed Voices* (Milkweed Editions), *descant: An Anthology of Fiction, Poetry, Essays 1956-1980* (Texas Christian University), *Mother of the Groom* (Distinctive Publishing), *I Am Becoming the Woman I've Wanted* (Papier-Mache Press), *I Name Myself Daughter and It Is Good* (Sophia Books), *Inheritance of Light* (University of North Texas Press), *New Texas '91, 2000, 2001* (Center for Texas Studies), *Proposing on the Brooklyn Bridge* (Poetworks/Grayson), *Southwest* (Red Earth Press), *Texas in Poetry* (Center for Texas Studies), *Texas in Poetry2* (Texas Christian University Press), *Texas Poetry Calendar 2005* (Flying Cow Press), *Texas Poetry Calendars 2010, 2011* (Dos Gatos Press), *This Place in Memory* (University of North Texas Press), *Valleysong* (Texas Rio Writers), *Zoo Poems* (Pudding House)

Poetry Volumes

Bonds. Jan Epton Seale. riverSedge poetry series (No. 1), second edition, 1981.
Sharing the House. Jan Epton Seale. riverSedge poetry series (No. 3), 1982.
A Quartet: Texas Poets in Concert. Jan Epton Seale, R.S. Gwynn, Naomi Shihab Nye, and William Virgil Davis. University of North Texas Press; Texas Poets Series (No. 2), 1990.
The Yin of It. Jan Epton Seale. Pecan Grove Press, 2000.

CONTENTS

Innocent of Reason

Bonds

Sharing the House

Midcourse

Believing is Seeing

Persons Solid and Magical

South by Southwest

Introduction to the Second Edition

Lately I have been thinking about how our poems choose us. Forever before, a poem does not exist, and then, some day when we least expect it, or conversely, are fervently entreating it, there it is.

We can attend workshops, study the great poetry masters, graduate from writing programs, write with fair ease a villanelle or a pantoum, and yet, and yet, the poems we write are, in a sense, the peculiar ones we are destined to write.

Poem-making chose me early on, before I knew how to get the words on paper. Recalling that time, I think of myself holding my hand to one ear, rocking back and forth, repeating the line that had startled itself into my young brain, and coaxing the next thought out of hiding—always in meter and rhyme.

Like all good mysteries, we come to a place where we are stumped by the origin and the urgency of the poems we write. Of course, we can trace our subjects by our genes, inheritance, experiences, emotions, and our close observations of the world and its stories around us.

But why does a certain idea tap us on the shoulder, clear its throat, positively insist that we pay it attention? When we do, one thing leads to another. More ideas come forward. Do they fit with the original one? Or do they demand their own poems? At some point, we simply stretch out our hands to receive our unique parcel, the thrill and the work of poetry.

If we're lucky, the mystery travels through us and renews itself in the alert listener or reader, the enjoyer, if you will—as that person receives the poem. And if we poets would be generous practitioners of our art, we will often position ourselves as the benevolent hearers of others' poems.

But it doesn't do any good for a poet to envy another poet's gift. That is time wasted. We will always owe a great debt to the masters, our poetic forebears. And we may learn from our contemporary favorites, enjoying them to the fullest, even thrilling to them, but we must not believe for one minute that the exact same talent can be ours. Those admired poets have their unique gifts. We need to become, and remain, their affirming audience, not their jealous critics or adoring sycophants.

It's good for a poet's soul to be generous to other poets, to lift them to the light so that poets and their audiences everywhere can find each other, taking deep pleasure and solace in the art. It is not good to spend time *yearning* to write poems that are not in us, that are not our givens. Better to spend that time striving to receive our subjects, along with their treatments, the ways they desire to be born and live in the world of thought. Better to surrender to the mysterious claims on our own minds and souls.

Regardless of our age or experience, all of us have plenty to write about. The young have yet to put in the hours of living, but they have their energy and enthusiasm to bolster what experience they do have. Their elders have a vast set of years to draw on, as much as their concentration and life circumstances will allow.

Reflecting on the poems in this volume, I have little explanation for many here which chose me as their amanuensis over a thirty-eight-year period. By that I mean that they seem at this vantage *whole*, or *done—* irrevocable and inevitable.

And now, with this second edition comes a sampling of a dozen new poems from the emerging decade under the heading "South by South-west." Of course I've written many more poems on other subjects in the last few years, but these, which I first thought of labeling "Location, Location" bunched themselves, hefty enough to insist on harmonizing with the earlier themed sections. They bring the poems in the volume back to the landing pad of the first section, "Crossing to Either Side." Yes, after forty years, I am still here, deep in the feet of Texas.

Some may conclude that with the importance I have given in my writing to my homeland—really almost an outpost, just a few miles from Mexico—that I should be branded a 'regional writer.' It seems to me that that old limiting label has about played itself out, but if not, I gladly submit, observing that all writers really are 'regional', if we're paying attention to what's going on around us, if we address our surrounds, and if we would accept the givens of our lives, one of which is our habitat.

When *The Wonder Is* first appeared, a wise friend opined that I had not dated each poem, to make more chronological sense of the journey to my readers and show my progression as a poet. I understood his point.

I know generally in which period of my life a poem was written, and many indicate that by their subject matter or by when they were first published, but there were years when poem-making and living the outer life ran pell-mell over each other. With a family, a teaching career, and a gregarious nature, I often struggled to find a lone place in my days for writing, much less to record the date when I pronounced a poem finished. Some general periods are obvious, for example, when parenting or academics were in the ascendancy; likewise, the women's movement, war (take your pick which one), and environmental awareness.

Am I embarrassed by any of my poems written twenty or thirty years ago? Okay, yes, a few that are published, and some hidden carefully in my study in a folder marked "early poems." Still, here in my eighth decade, I am surprised that I am more satisfied than not with poems written so long ago. Then, I was who I was; the poems were what they were. It may be that, after all, the center holds. Our poems keep insisting we claim them because, again, they are the ones we are uniquely meant to write.

These days I feel wiser and more cautious, in certain ways tougher and in others more tender. The young radicalized passionate poem-maker has become more introspective and moderate, more accepting. She is sometimes alarmed and certainly more grasping as the future shrinks. She is still often confused but always amazed by life, and ever willing still to embrace it.

Let me express here my gratitude for the faith of Guida Jackson, a fine writer and former owner and editor of Panther Creek Press, who published this volume in its original form in 2005. She generously gave consent for this second edition, sculpted by Jerry Craven, another fine writer and editor, of Ink Brush Press. In an age when poetry is sometimes treated as an anachronism, such encouragement as these have given is a vote for the vibrancy and power of the art. To accept the donnée of our poems is one gift. To take up the cause of poetry by shepherding others' poems into publication is also a startling and unique gift.

There's plenty of wonder to go around.

Jan Seale
2012 Texas Poet Laureate

The wonder is
how a tree scribbles on the sky
how the sky plagiarizes without shame
how the earth turns
page after page of grass
and we know this to be
the only handwriting on the wall

Crossing to Either Side

Subtropical

The southeast wind brings the smell of Gulf.
The orchid tree blushes a hundred blooms.
The cactus can't decide, pink or yellow,
all the while hiding its fruit like a girl.

I walk the circle, where the setting sun
and a cluster of palms plan a postcard.
It's a street with escape routes
but who would want them?

Someone needs to tell the woodpecker
it's evening, time to knock off.
A crowd of starlings is making
Susan's cottonwood shiver.

Homeward, I drag two dried fronds.
In the alley, a dead grackle,
still vain in his amethyst feathers
discovers me and grins.

I fold him in the fronds.
They are two of a kind,
a small funeral mound
against this excess life.

After Sunday

        on the plaza
starlings shimmer the laurels,
sustain the love of *novios*
parting to separate beds
at midnight.
Later, the cold before dawn
brings low laughter and feet
running light on the stones.

They emerge beneath the knitted trees,
young waiters newly freed from drunks
in well-lighted places. Now a catcall
confirmed by clapping, low words.
In twos and threes they jump the steps
to the street, their white shirts
luminous as angels by lamp's light.
They pass under open windows,
are gone.
        Only a moment, *mágico*,
a dream handed the roused sleeper
to lie quietly in, try to recall.

Were they here, these boys,
their small night joy published
on the starlings' wings at dawn
as the whole world's joy?

Still Life With Migrating Bees
(on the road to Ciudad Victoria)

Water rushes from a pipe
near the small girl,
her navy skirt pressed,
her white blouse starched.
A woman in a red sweater
waits with her.
A worker in a hat
sits across the road.
He is either watching them or not.
They are either watching him or not.
A killer bee trap hangs nearby.
Does it contain bees? No one knows.

The girl will soon catch the bus.
The woman will return to her fire.
The worker will wait out his life
until afternoon.
Then the girl will return,
her mother come to greet her,
the two walk out of the worker's sight,
no one left to observe him
except the bees, if they exist.

Landfall

Palm, ash, cottonwood have entered
a dance marathon, hour after hour
slam-dunking and foxtrotting
to the latest steps of wind.

We alone without anemometers
judge the storm by what we see
out our taped windows. If the trees
are upright, so are we.

Morning light finds us dragging
branches to the alley, raking
leaves out of season. We mourn what
we could not know needed prayers:

a strip of shingles vanished,
our ruling patio lizard banged dead,
the hibiscus stark naked,
a grand mesquite felled at the knees.

We entertain the craziness that,
if we had only known to hope,
to pray them, we could have saved them.
So the lesson goes to heart:

close monitoring of inner weather—
sunrises or gray rain,
hurricane warning, or the flag of sex
waving its pretty head.

Our hearts, untended, die.
We begin again the vigil:
Sorrow. Retribution. Passion. Love.
They must all be accounted for.

Big Bend: Lion Warning
a found poem

A lion has been frequenting this area
It could be aggressive toward humans

If you see a lion
Pick up small children
Stand together
Appear large
Wave hands and shout
Throw stones or sticks
Report sighting to ranger

Do not
Show fear
Crouch down
Run away

To a late local environmentalist

You went away to die, like an ailing pet
we search the neighborhood for.
I had a new book for you,
one about our river lands,
the precious ribbon of life
you took so personally,
worked at as an antidote
for the slow poison taking you.
The book was inscribed,
"To ____, friend of all Valley creatures,
with my love and admiration."

Today I take it from its mailer,
cut out its inscription page,
tape on a note: Damaged.
Back on the shelf.
I hate the envelope,
its accusing "Return to Sender" finger,
start to toss it, but
you wouldn't want me wasting a tree.
Remember how we held that funeral
for a cluster of palms uprooted,
replaced by a discount shoe store?

Just now at dawn the red-crowned parrots
make their daily flight over my house,
their sudden hilarious screeching
saying it's *el primer día* of their world,

saying you rest in *el primer día*
of your new habitat, that you smile,
seeing the bobcat hides in his
necessary brush along the Rio Grande.

Action Shot

The master of this house tells how he loved the motion
of those he killed—the way the wild turkey
spread his wings, the pheasant held his beak high,
the javelina charged. He got the wolf
with foot posed midair, and a bobcat snarling.
Now deer burst through his walls sniffing the air,
their fine neck muscles bulging, a little of the hair
of the chest sprouting from the walnut mount,
showing how the hair turns, takes new direction
toward the underbelly, past the once-beating heart.

Fence

Dawn and a ripple crosses its cracks,
stippled negative like a glissando—
in the alley a *viejito* gathering cardboard,
his scarved *esposa* reaping cans, pie tins.
Later dragonflies balance, take a reading,
cats claw up the wobbling braces,
surprise lizards in toehold romance.
It's love and death in the afternoon.
Evenings, pigeons land light as tissues.
The moon shows a possum sacking up and over.

One night in spring the fence will come alive,
its stiffened spine strain for light.
In the first high wind it will break ground,
groan, move off in its own gray vision
toward the river.

The Pigs of Mexico

The ones tame as dogs
root through hot coals,
lounge on porches,
come at beckoning.
Others force their snouts
in cracks of concrete stalls,
wear their pronged collars
like the medieval tortured.

Chicharrones,
gorditos, aceite,
tocino, hamon y huevos,
puerco con everything—
the names of the eaten
are flavorful.
They crackle,
fry well,
run down the chin.

Those *marranos*!
They're the only ones left
to celebrate
the fat of the land.

Traveling North: The Rules

Mile 49: Ladies and gentlemen,
United States Immigration Checkpoint coming
up! Please have your documentation ready.
¡Damas y caballeros tambien!

Now there must be a neatening—
all things vertical, horizontal, squared:
hats removed, hair smoothed, hats replaced;
pant legs worked back down the thighs;
boot toes polished on backs of opposing calves;
lipstick checked; long hair slung-brushed;
babies taken off breast; blouses closed;
waking of older children, Sit up!

Now the *papeles*, always the *papeles*:
from shirt pockets, billfolds, purses,
bosoms, boot tops, jean pockets.
You unfold your *papeles*
or take your card from its holder:
Do you look like your picture?
Hold your life steady;
practice holding your future
steady in your hands.

The driver will pull into the port.
Stop talking. Cross yourself.
Immigration Checkpoint! He will climb down.
Look clean; look bright;
look like your picture ID.

La Migra will board.
(*La Migra* is not kidding.)
Have your *papeles* ready.
¡Buenas tardes! He will speak
kind to the *viejos* on the front seat.

La Migra starts down the aisle:

You citizens?
You?
This your bag?
La Migra looks at each passenger,
takes the *papeles*, studies it,
pats the seatback as he passes.

La Migra checks the bathroom.
(You better not be in it.)
Now he returns, his boots sounding.
He will be looking for telltale signs.
(You better not be handing your *papeles*
back to your friend just yet.)

It is almost over. Everyone is fine...
—wait! He's asking that gringo hippie,
What you doing down in the Valley?

Nothing, man!

That *bolillo*! He doesn't know the rules!
For that he goes with *La Migra*,
keeps us all here, waiting.

Would he empty, please,
the contents of his purple nylon bag
onto the table? Another guy comes.
They take up a book and shake it
like something might fall out.
They examine another object.
Someone looking safely out the window:
Eh, *estúpidos*! That's a *capo* for a guitar,
not a roach clip! The bus laughs.

The gringo hippie is allowed back.

When the bus is under way again,
food will break out all over:
empanadas, gorditas, fruta,

17

Cocas, Topo Chico.

¡Gracias a Dios! a *viejita*
will breathe it.
An old cowboy will hear.
¡Palabra! No kidding!

South Texas Mini-drama
(with apology to Dylan Thomas)

Setting
   one late August morning

Characters
      one common grackle—
         song like crunched paper bag
      one cicada—
         song like inner ear trouble

Act I
      bird catches cicada on lawn
      cicada loudly sings

Act II
      bird immobilizes cicada
      by eating wings
      cicada loudly sings

Act III
      bird harasses cicada
      by eating head
      cicada loudly sings

Act IV
      bird eats sing

Epilogue
      cicadas go not gentle
      into their goodnights.

The business boys of Reynosa

are constant as grass,
own elbows and knees of earth,
invent a new brown for eyes.
They fill socks suspended
inside their shirts with pesos
from windshield cleanings,
chiclet sales, spit shoeshines,
from message deliveries.
On the side, they trade
in string and old toy cars.
They line up to practice English,
"One dime?" and "You like?"
The granite *patriota* in the plaza
where they meet means *nada*,
but they themselves have plans
to be great. When the sock is
half full, they pee in the shadows
and start home to mother and sister.
They enter the *casita*, eat cold tacos,
lie across the foot of the bed.
In their dreams they hear matin bells,
cocks crowing too soon.

Big Bird Comes to the Valley in 1976

The color was white, silver, gray, brown, dark brown, black.
The height was four, five, six feet; the wingspan, twenty.
Otherwise, the bird was hairy, feathered, bald. In the pictures
drawn at school, there was the face of a bat, pig, monkey, man—
with pointed ears, eagle's beak, stork's bill, silvery red eyes.
"Pteranodon" and "pterasaurus" were librarians' nightmare.

The creature left footprints, hovered over a lagoon, hissed,
ransacked a tavern, terrified policemen, pursued children,
disappeared into a canal, perched on the Chevrolet company,
attacked two men (making one of them hot where it touched),
gave an unearthly noise, snapped its beak, ran into the brush.

There were T-shirts in four sizes and a song on a record—
the flip side an interview, old Japanese monster movies,
offered rewards and counter-rewards, vigilante groups formed,
words from the law on trigger-happiness, on endangered species,
talks about self-defense, bounty hunting, international animals.

At the end, the bird let itself be filmed in an orchard
with fifty people surrounding. Then the legend flew away.
The 6 p.m. news showed a mild blue heron gazing about.
The next day, its published demise: "Legend of Bird is Dead."
Soon the TV station had tossed the film, for more space—
(reports of drug hauls, bodies found in the Rio,
deaths of the prominent, arrests of molesters, murderers).

Then a haze clouded the eyes so the people no longer saw
the jabiru, crane, wood stork, brown pelican, condor,
and especially the great blue heron; even though these birds,
one or all, were here, in our midst: even though they came
to restore rumor, debate, declamation, the art of gossip,
the plucking of guitars, chills, *cuentos de las lechuzas*,
upstanding hair on the nape, children curved with respect
into the laps of the *viejitos* on front porches at evening.

Guerrero Viejo

In 1953, the government moved the residents of Guerrero
to higher ground to make way for Falcon Lake, created
by a new international dam on the Rio Grande.
                                        travel brochure

What mean ye by these stones?
                        Joshua 4:6

These stones, ruined, meant a dozen border boom towns,
fields of cabbage, onions, sugar cane, no floods.
These stones meant fishermen could use
the bell tower of Nuestra Señora del Refugio, 200 years old,
like the eye of a needle through which to thread their boats.
And what's it all for now—the meaning of these stones?
That they can lie for 40 years in a grave of water,
then smile a gleaming sunlit smile at rain gods' jokes.
That the snail makes its bed in the charcoal pit;
that the cactus mimes the crab; that Our Lady of Refuge
looms high in the air again, protecting pigeons.

An old door, faithful to its hinges through years of water,
squeaks out a complaint to drought.
Cows graze in the *colegio*, wander roofless classrooms,
do not try to learn any message from lost schoolboys.

Matins, still dark

a town first awakens the people with bells
a town calls loud for God with bells
a town speaks glossolalia in bells
a town attends a party of bells
a town makes love to bells
a town delirious in bells
a town chatting in bells
a town cross with bells
a town sad with bells

a town in a final competition of bells
loose, crying, murdering with bells
a town, town, town
a few bells
two bells
bell

Borderwomen Triptych

I. Gentle conversation

My grandmother was named Malinche.
Mine was named Melinda.
My mother was frightened by a lunar eclipse.
My mother ate too many pickles and strawberries.
Once I was almost killed by a flying tortilla.
I was seriously grazed by a slice of white bread.
My family had a porción from the King of Spain.
My family had a bunk on the Mayflower.
I spent my childhood in the campo.
I spent my childhood on a vacant lot.
My maiden name is Garza.
My maiden name is Jones.
My married name is Garcia.
My married name is Johnson.
I am the color of nutmeg.
I am the color of cream.

II. When the missionary feminists came

The evangelical feminists came to the border.
They flew in from the Northeast, phoning collect
to say they were bringing our salvation.
We told them we had a women's course.
They asked us where the hell
were our consciousness groups.
We told them we had Sociology-and-Gender.
They objected: the course was not woman-taught.
We thought—in our polite border way
of thinking instead of saying—
that if they would only capitulate
and comb their hair,
or mute their nipples a bit,
the townspeople would talk to them.
But they walked too fast,

and made too many phone calls,
and took out a citizen's warrant
to arrest our only OB-Gyn for maleness.
They interrupted us when
we tried to answer their questions,
telling us our accents
were amusing but unintelligible.
They wouldn't say who kept them
in cigarettes or the biggest hotel in town.
They wanted to fit us with diaphragms,
extract our menstrual blood
along the canal banks or field rows.
Thank God they finally went home
with all their hard-won facts.
We cleaned up the rubble of our nerves,
whistling cheerfully like janitresses
in gymnasiums running wide mops
over a post-game mess.
We said they meant well,
that it was fun having new voices
in our midst—
and felt as shabby and provincial
and put-down as we did
before they came to the border
bearing our salvation.

III. To the difference-mongers

They tell us to pay close attention
to our heritage
They tell us when we answer please
use only yes or no
They tell us to notice
how our separate cultures
treat their men their children
their old their poor
how we eat different foods
celebrate our holidays differently
They tell us different cultures

simply differ in treatment of women
They tell us not to deal in trivia:
equal pay equal work equal loads
Just be one of your culture's women
Don't make waves along the *rio.*
But for that Rio Grande, the *Río Bravo,*
there is a counterpart
an underground river of lives
a dark murmuring passage
manzanilla tea and black coffee
a ribbon running sweet between women
a catacomb of sister rooms
a tape measure a lifeline
a zipper a scarf a necklace
the fused spine of two cultures,
we who are Maria Guadalupes
and Mary Louises
saying we are women first
more alike than different
saying we will hang together
because we won't hang separate
saying family of woman
saying border of what?

Train Kills 6 Sleeping on Tracks

Their deaths anecdotal,
all that we know, presumed:

Which said he would awaken, sure he would,
he always slept lightly at home in Mexico?

And which said, No, no, he'd stand guard?

Was one persuasive in the immigrants' tale
that snakes never cross railroad tracks?

And another who said he did not believe it,
but if the others did...?

Whose dream cleverly worked into the plot
first the vibration and then the sound?

Did any think to save himself by putting
his head back down,

Some one of them have time to *adios* the future?

Could the farthest from the approaching train
hear at first "a loud slapping," as did a man nearby?

Well, and did any snakes silently crawl over them,
in their sleep—that is, before the big one?

Christmastide: the Texican Border

Mild, sheep weather,
star-harboring skies,
a travellers' moon;

stones to pile up,
sit upon, make a fence,
roll away from a tomb;

cicadas singing glorias,
flowering olives for prayer,
fig trees cursed and blessed;

Palma Christi for donkey feet,
for sparrow homes,
for Solomon's sweets;

the passion flower of cacti,
sand to write a message in,
posadas to journey in hope;

and a river, wide and deep,
where, crossing to either side,
we are baptized anew.

Opened Letters

Salutation Attempt 1976

Dear Person:
    Dear Human:
        Dear Androgyne:

Dear Unmentionable Crotch:
    Dear Secret-from-the-knees-up:
        Dear Concaved or -vexed Chest:

Dear Sensitive Brute:
    Dear Brutally Sensitive:
        Dear Different-in-qualities-but-not-value:

Dear Inferior-in-superiority:
    Dear Superior-in-inferiority:
        Dear Exactly Alike:

Not-so-dear—
    Two-legged—
        To-Whom-or-What-this-may-or-may-not-concern.

Ovulation

An idea maturing late last month
floated toward the heart;
it sent small stabbing signals
gave a slight fever
and a certain sense of desire.

Finding not a thing along the way
to couple with and bloom nor any
alternate openings or staying powers
it gave up.
        Next morning
it was gone by way of a schedule.

Self-help Manual

I. Confessional poets

Grasp the front flaps of yourself firmly
Wait for a group of people laughing and unconcerned
Leap out with a samurai cry, planting your feet wide
Show every part that's been giving you trouble
Do not think of the future

II. Lyric poets

Announce a weekend retreat devoted to trancing
Lay in a supply of sangria and gum
Retrieve CDs from friends
Make a smokey bonfire of punctuation and syntax
Say prayers to Saint Joyce and Saint Hopkins
Fall in love with your voice box

III. Mood poets

Awake mindless
Brew a cup of anything
Discover leftovers of an old love affair under bed
Stare out the window at birds, grass, trees
Begin the poem "Today, I must write a poem"
End the poem "I know not why the rain falls."

My Big Chief Is Trying to Speak at the Writers' Retreat

So far, this new yellow writing tablet,
beckoning as a daffodil,
smooth as a dog's tongue,
patient to the day of judgment,
sunshine with sky blue lines,
drug of choice to the pen,
safe haven for homeless words
has
lined a rain-soaked deck chair,
stanched a leak in the cabin ceiling,
received a berry deposit from a bird,
tendered a sign: Squirrel Loose in Bathroom,
saved the environment from gum,
collected this list.

Things I Did Not Say at a Junior High Poetry Workshop

Any other way is better to get loved.
Gargle with the following:
      "Relationships are more important than poems.
       Poems are more important than relationships."
Whichever gags you, abide by the other.

A poem is not a 40-hour week,
is better than Sominex,
is equivalent to a burp or dandruff
at rodeos, beauty salons, grocery stores,
family reunions.

A poem, read in the afternoon among furs,
will have the little foxes crying real tears;
if coddled, may run into the bushes,
may lie down grinning and dead as a possum.

Poems have been known to hide in songs
and toilet compartments,
can become mouthfuls of lozenges.

Sometimes a poem burns the eyes
like a solar eclipse, blinds the poet.
Look to the sense of it
through smoked lens.

Including the above,
all generalizations about poems
are false.

Samuel Taylor Coleridge, I Hear You

*At this moment he was unfortunately called out by
a person on business from Porlock, and detained by
him above an hour, and on his return to his room, found,
to his no small surprise and mortification...all the rest had
passed away.*

Preface to "Kubla Khan"

I got out of bed in the dark
with the most moist poem
I had ever thought.
It felt right.
It smelled right
and was holding still.
I turned on the light
because obviously,
I said,
I can't see the lines
unless there's light.
I found a pencil.
The thing immediately
jumped down,
crawled under the bed
and refused to come out.
All night it made
obscene lumps
in my mattress.

Riff

At the neck of the word,
the tube that gets no respect,
at the neck of the word,
no, not entirely the head,
with its careful round thoughts,
its cerebral priss,
nor yet in the body,
a nonsense of sounds—
awful palpitations
and twitchings,
ague and gut growl—
not that either,
but at the neck of the word,
where brain and gut meet,
where meaning and moaning
smooth together,
conjoin,
form a tunnel
piping what
we're trying to say—
Hallow! We call—
Hallow! It's dark in here
in here
at the neck of the word.
On the verge of
the truest thing
we've ever spoken
and the chopping block:
this place,
the neck of the word.

The Critic Helps the Poet

The first 3 lines of this poem
are too prosaic. The second
sentence jerks—tone changes.

DO NOT READ THE ABOVE.

Lines 4-7 show some development
of the idée fixe but
wander too much—thus
chatty and indulgent.

STRIKE LL. 4-7.

Any images coming up are
1) self-serving
2) too easy
3) mannered
4) trivial
5) creaking
6) offensive to my taste.

OMIT ALL QUALIFYING 1) THROUGH 6).

The ending is lame and inept,
sentimental and uncontrolled.

DO NOT END THIS POEM.

P.S. It's a marvelous poem
(tho' not terribly ambitious.)

So? Art!

It was mid-term, and not a research-
ical mouse had scampered across
the assistant professor's desk--
oh, true, he had had a musty whiff about
Kafka's phantasmagoria once
and another time, seen just the tip,
the brown tip of a Wordsworth existentialism,
but nothing worth calling off classes for.
One day there appeared a large contraption
in the professor's mailbox. It said,

    VICTORY MOUSETRAP

with a note from the dean that
all requests for tenure and promotion
were due in a week.

The assistant professor went straight
to his office, locked the door,
stuck out his tongue, attached the VICTORY.
He sat on his hands 'til the carillon
rang the next quarter hour.
He took the trap off,
felt his huge purple tongue,
let one large plop ripening
in his left eye fall on his lapel,
and put paper in the typewriter:

Lygaeid

Blackbirds alighting on curtains
eschatological dreaming
if I will ever
feel more of the
turgid bumping of the
death cart o robespierre

there is a turning and a
gyrating and an improper
unlucid feeling in my heart
last night the dream I had
turned me over in my bed
that's how I know it's worth
turning over to the world

The professor smiled, (but his tongue still hurt)
took the paper from the typewriter.
And started over. This was the revision.
He double-spaced, was careful to eliminate
the capital letter, wondered if "had" and "bed"
would irritate the editor.

He made the lines a bit less rhythm-
ic and triple-spaced   between   words.
He hiccuped once and it seemed to have
such a true meaning with what he was saying
he added it and hoped the editor would notice
that it made the line dactyllic hexameter.

A few pau-
ses (incasehewaseveraskedto giveitina reading)
and he was finished.
He folded the paper carefully,
clipped it in VICTORY
and left his office.

He would have whistled
on the way to the dean's office
but it hurt to curl his tongue.

Lecturing on Sylvia Plath

I shut my eyes and all the class drops dead;
I lift my lids and there they are again.
(I wish I'd made them up inside my head.)

I try to make them see that what she said
and what she did were not summarily insane.
I shut my eyes and all the class drops dead.

They drum their pens at babies pickled, tulips red,
list 3 important points on Esther's pain.
(I wish I'd made them up inside my head.)

The boys stretch and see themselves in bed
with girls who haven't poems on the brain.
I shut my eyes and all the class drops dead.

Studying sickies—you sure can't get ahead;
lots of women with kids don't complain.
(I wish I'd made them up inside my head.)

Black stars and rooks and bell jars are too sad.
Poets are nuts. To kill yourself is sin.
I shut my eyes and all the class drops dead.
(I wish I'd made them up inside my head.)

An Open Letter to Composition Students

Strive to make your writing unified, coherent, and complete.
                                                    composition manual

Today we are talking of compound sentences;
tomorrow, the paragraph; next week, the essay.
Sometime I will ask you for papers.
Sometime I will walk between the rows
collecting your writing. You will fold the paper
and write your name on the front.
You will toss it to me, or schmooze it to me,
or put it in the wrong stack on my desk.

We reach an uneasy peace about comma splices,
assignments for tomorrow, the objective case,
the thesis sentence. You stay bound in your notes.
I stay clipped in my grade book.
You hand in bits of yourself.
I pass back minims of myself.
You need to hate me a little
because it is something students do.
I need to hate you a little
because it is something teachers do.

But someday after I post your final grade
and you see it, grab your temples and swear,
or grab your friend and leap like a glad fool
there in the narrow hall, someday later we may meet
on a covered walkway between classes.
Do not be surprised if I comma your elbows
lightly with my hands, my former student
with thick hair and white teeth,
in jeans and sloganed T-shirt. Do not be surprised
if I tell you, there on the covered walkway,
without my grade book and in less than 500 words,
that you are unified, coherent, and complete.

The Brain Has a Mind of Its Own

My friend across town, making his bi-weekly call,
states a truth: Our neurons are out to get us.

Clanging away, I say.

Those synapses are hoses, he says;
they haul out the big ones when I get up to pee,
just super-trash from conversations the night before.

Insinuations, I say, overstatements, neglects, lies.

Barreling down the pike, he says;
you're not apt to get a decent thought at 2:30 a.m.

It's very seldom a satisfaction, I say,
like love remembered, or a tiny emotional lottery won.

Or like the best dinner I ever cooked, he says.

Like everything is actually and really going to turn out
all right after all, I say.

Like by dawn's early light, you can count on big ideas
and little or no interference to get them done, he says.

Bookmark

Thank you for waiting patiently until we return,
red lace of Switzerland, green leather of Ireland,
papier mâché with sloe-eyed natives harvesting.
Still, you have a life of your own, a job to envy.

Who would not like, hour after hour, to be pressed
with ideas in the den, feel the tickle of feathers
from a coffee table hawk, be allowed to snigger
at a bathroom cousin shut in an academic journal?

Plastic Pharaoh new-dug from the museum store,
embroidered red poppy of an August birthday,
laminated rosemary from a Northwest garden,
tiny zarape migrating from the Mexican market,

placemat laid for a dinner of paragraphs,
rooster crowing from the edge of the page,
prisoner condemned to the medieval press
or a long, long wait on the chopping block,

transformed from souvenir to consort
of the best words in their best order,
what's it like to hold a place in time and space,
to separate yesterday from tomorrow?

And what's not to envy in your life—
to be lifted with love, fingered, nibbled, held close,
and, when all is known for now,
put back between the sheets?

Innocent of Reason

Playing the Flute for the TMR Class

Children admitted to the Trainable Mentally Retarded
program must have some minimal communication
ability in the form of either speech or gestures.
                    education guidelines

They stumbled down their barracks steps
and bombed my car with sighs and shouts,
ancient children set for a lark.
I went smoothed and fingered, lingered on
and lifted up, up to their porch
patterned with sun on chicken wire
into their ripe dark classroom where
"doll" and "book" swam trainably abandoned
on the board until their teacher
came in flowered smock and quickly taught
the meaning of a semi-circle,
her Christmas angel eyes bidding me unafraid.

Sweating hands pressed every key,
worked all the levers, stroked
each millimeter of silver then let me
put it to my mouth and gave my fingers
grudging space upon the keys. So
came the holy Yankee Doodle spirit
marching and clapping and singing,
rolling on to bird calls, both hoot owls
and Pastoral Symphony warblers, fire truck sirens
convulsive and night trains whistling.

Batman! Batman! they were crying
and with the half-steps of his tune one climbed
on a chair and soared off, we following like
a thousand evening bats at cave entrance,

rising, so we did it. Jingle Bells Michael
Row Your Boat Ashore Oh Susannah Don't Mission
Impossible Jesus Loves Me Home On the
Range The Real Thing Two Little Ducks:
it was time.

I dried my silver pipe and broke it
magically to pieces, laying it to sleep
in the Cinderella velvet of the box,
while they said it was pretty and they loved me
and why did I have to go? But I did,
assisted by a score of unmeditated caresses,
driving away too much alone, leaving
the only Holy Pied Spirit singing and kissing the wind.

Chapel

The soldier's ears sprout pink below the hair
cut one-half inch to army regulation;
they scoop up headgearsful of words
the prayer is programming
for later meditation in the helicopter
squatting among the enemy.
Responsive reading number twenty-nine
calls his attention to a speck
of oily stuff beneath his thumbnail
which demands the time spanning the offertory.
When next, "Praise God From Whom All Blessings"
sends him to attention on football legs,
back like a ramrod, does he not look like Jesus
of stained-glass ascension?
The sermon is quite long: "How to Be Brave."
Between his ears he contemplates his grave.

Feast Day at Jémez

I.
We are the lucky ones, *bolillos* invited to Joyce's pueblo.
It is August 2, the Feast of Our Lady of the Angels
with the Old Pecos Bull Dance, the day donated in 1838
by eighteen poor Pecos come to winter with the Jémez.
Certain outsiders may visit, but only friends may eat.
We have been designated friends.

Chiles dry on the *viga* ends. We enter, admire the den,
wood-panelled, added to the stucco front.
Joyce, a registered nurse, has laid a fine table.
We sit with a family from Isleta, but,
corrects the mother, she herself is an Acoma.
Their girls are shy, curling into their chairs,
dabbling their pumpkin bread in red juice.
One stretches her peasant blouse over her mouth
when spoken to. Their father is a water engineer.
He does his work according to his master's degree
from the university—he is not a kachina!
The mother has tried speaking to the girls in Keresan
but they are learning more Tiwa, living in Isleta.

We drink Koolaid from jelly glasses, pass the woven basket
filled with breads from the outdoor oven,
eat chunks of venison simmering in liquid fire.
In the kitchen, Joyce dips more beans from the Crockpot.
It is a Christmas present from her husband Buddy.
She can't be watching a famous Jémez beanpot all day—
she's at the government health service.
There is fruit cocktail pudding for dessert.
Joyce's son Junior is off at the kick-stick races.
He has fussed because they canceled Little League.
Buddy went out early to cut branches from the Rio Jémez.
He sends his regrets but will see us after the dancing.
They are of the *tabösh*, the squash order—
Look for Junior dusted with yellow among the dancers.

We linger at table while the children flip the TV
atop which sits the *Virgen* protected by a stuffed owl.
On the wall a deer head examines the colored photo
of Joyce's brother in football uniform.

We pick at the crumbs, have one more bite of meat.
We are talking and talking.
The spirits settle in around us.

II.
Joyce gives us directions. She will be along later.
We go with the Romeros from Isleta and Acoma,
taking our time picking our way down the hillside,
holding back a little when a dog growls, a face appears.

Coming out between dwellings, we are unprepared
for the space, a plaza of sand big as a soccer field.
At the far end Our Lady of the Angels sits in blessing
of a yucca shelter. Transported from the church,
she is comfortable among crosses, flowers.
This is the last time we will see her.

The turquoise order flows in. These are the *tsúnta tabösh*.
They concern themselves with the sprouting of plants.
They are the winter group.

Somewhere down near Our Lady of the Angels,
the *cacique* gives the signal and the drumming begins.
A choir of men, the old in polyester and squash blossoms,
the young in jeans and boots, moves out to the chant
of the Walatowa. The square is awash in color, motion,
like a camouflaged beast flushed from hiding.
Slow feet beginning, sway of bodies, branches waving.
Girls and women smothered in sashes, sacques, rebozos,
vests, leggings, crowned in turquoise headpieces;
boys and men in breech cloths, shells like bullet belts
crossing their chests, coyote skins tied to their waists,
fir branches bouncing like show ponies' tails.
Thousands of bells say their prayers in unison.

The dancers do not smile, do not recognize anyone.
This dance is not for tourists. No pictures.
Heat shimmers. The desert praises this lake of color.
We stand bleached to the bone with envy.

III.
The dancers are taking a break.
One young man, glistening by now,
little streaks of blue dripping toward his navel
approaches a black-haired girl in the crowd.
She wears Gloria Vanderbilt jeans, carries a canvas purse.
They haven't seen each other since graduation.
How's she been?
Just fine.
What's he doing now?
Oh, he's a trainee at Sears in town.
Just out for the day, had to come do the dancing.
His father is calling.
She stands on her toes to kiss him,
careful not to touch his sweat.

IV.
Now the squash dancers take their place.
An old man in the chant group growls,
"Back! Back! Can't you see we need room?"
We can't see—don't know the divine plan
but stumble backward over each other,
humbled and guilt-stricken.
Buddy is in the squash chanters.
He greets us, goes solemnly to his work.
Some of the old men move their mouths
hardly at all, perhaps out of boredom,
perhaps to conceal their words from us.
Some of the younger watch the mouths of the old.
It is important to get it right, keep it right.

The drumming, the shuffling begin.
The chinking of bells. The nasal singing.
On and on. On and on. Seductive murmur.

The sun doesn't move all afternoon.
My friends leave for shade.
I look down; the tops of my feet are scorched.
I have not shifted for three hours.
Maybe I am planted.
Maybe this is how they insure the crops.

That night back in Albuquerque, in bed at last,
I wish the sunburn were pigment.
I wonder how to belong,
how to read the god that drums my heart.

Sand paints me to sleep.

Come Celebrate Another Early Snake

Now the serpent was more subtle than any beast
of the field which the Lord God had made.
Genesis 3:1

Come celebrate another early snake—
a garden dweller who did not proffer sin.
Say that being also tended earth's daybreak.

Tell of a woman who did not care to make
a meal of apples and share them with her kin.
Come celebrate another early snake.

Rumor a man who did not know soul-ache
for an odyssey beyond the garden's din.
Say that being also tended earth's daybreak.

Speak a serpent whose head man could not break,
nor mouth would bruise a man's achilles-skin.
Come celebrate another early snake.

A woman who did not have a thirst to slake
in any juice of tree that might have been—
say that being also tended earth's daybreak.

Know a snake that moved for love's own sake.
Say for Eden's viper was a twin.
Come celebrate another early snake.
Say that being also tended earth's daybreak.

How the Wax Churches of Los Aztecas Bloom

When the air is dry and the day not too hot too cold
when the table is brought and placed four-square
in the center of the *ejido* and on it a bowl of water

when the world has lasted another year *Gracias a Dios*
because La Virgen de la Inmaculada Concepción
has interceded for the village of Los Aztecas and
Our Lady's festival is set for the eighth of December

when reeds are gathered from beside the Rio Guayalejo
and left to ripen then stripped and made into bases
with rising walls saving space for windows and doors
all leading heavenward by towers to roofs and crosses

when three dies of mesquite are brought from the trunk
where they live out generations wrapped in rags
except for these their own feast days and
are soaked in water and watched over for a small while

when the dyed bee's wax in the copper pan over the fire
rouses from last year's lump but does not smoke
and by the goat-footed grace of the artisan
arrives safe at the table over the hard ground

when the children are assembled at a distance
a few boys with sticks against the curious pigs
the women in doorways their arms full of babies
their heads draped in dish towels against the sun

when Pánfilo Vázquez Fondón takes up a die
with his tongs and dips it in the sun of bee's wax
with help from the ghost of his mother
who has help from the ghost of her father
who practiced this art in San Luis Potosí

and when the face of the die is coated with wax

and quickly held high like a crucifix by Pánfilo
who then brings it down to his mouth and blows thrice
Padre   Hijo   Espíritu Santo
peels the wax like the membrane of a newborn
baptizes his child in the bowl and then dries it

when he has enough stacks of patterns and colors
and when his friend Tranquilina from Palmillas
delivers him her wax flowers and bells the art of which
she had to leave her unsympathetic husband in order to save

when Pánfilo assembles all this in the storage jacal
and with a small fire going outside begins to attach
the filigreed segments one by one to the reed frame
handling each piece of wax as a butterfly or hot coal
as a bird's egg as snow as a silk ribbon as a kiss
his breath hardly taken and never the eyes off the work

reaching out sideways to the boy who will be there
to place the new ember in his hand until the corner
of one piece hangs to the cane then fuses with another
its neighbor until there is a transept of bright pink

like the roses clutched to the breast of La Virgen
and twin belfries webbed green as the grass at her feet
the windows and doors a white lace of her reputation
the roof fashioned of Our Lady of Heaven's blue mantle

when the churches all forty are finished so that word is sent
for Señoras Zarate and Canales and Apolado to fetch them
each taking her own church away on her head

Pánfilo standing in the doorway smiling and sighing
Adiós mis jardincitos, watching his little gardens march
straightaway each made with a difference detectable
only to himself because he has pledged it to God

when at last the eighth of December comes with veneration
of La Virgen de la Inmaculada Concepción who makes all
that is good to happen the rest of the year in Los Aztecas

and Pánfilo's wax churches are seen on the heads
of the faithful in the *parada* amidst the standards floating
with ribbons and children bearing scarves and priests
with headpieces and dancers Aztecas and the statue of *La Virgen*

when the time is over for the divine grillwork
for the arches scallops webs eyelets curves flowers
for the angles windows doors roofs and bells

and Pánfilo sits late in the night rubbing his eyes seeing
inside them his churches high on the heads of the faithful
in the brilliant midday how beautiful how beautiful
the *jardincitos* of Los Aztecas this year how beautiful

when Pánfilo has allowed his heart to soar to heaven
in the arms of La Virgen de la Inmaculada Concepción

then and only then does he give the sign
for the small greedy hands to tear the lace
from the frameworks throwing all into piles of color
breaking the frameworks of reeds to feed the fires
all the while Pánfilo hearing the laughter of destruction

it is then he melts down the mounds of lace to store
the lumps in cool jars sleeping away from the light
thinking how next year he will lay the fire
how he will stir the wax clods into swirling sky

how his hands will become the hands of the sower
scattering the seeds of sacrifice on Our Lady's altar
new and more beautiful churches offered up to her
these little gardens of his heart pleasing her

each piece of lace hearing the echo of its mother
out of the cold lump heating over the fire
each reed hearing from the crackling bonfire
of death its father of the year before

the freshest and most beautiful of bouquets springing
with gratitude and entreaty new ever new.

Faces in Everything

Lately, he's been seeing faces—
the side of the spoon rack,
the quilt early morning,
rain leaks on the ceiling tiles—
they're all folks.

Outdoors is not immune either—
visages in the shrubbery,
a little girl in the hibiscus,
a gnome peering out of the birdbath,
the oak glaring from across the street.

He does not tell her all—
too many, he says, and besides,
it would scare her:
the hordes they fly through 5 miles up,
the crowds she's entertaining in their house,
the ladies taking a bath with him.

In the Church at Mier

Shadow of Christ on the stone wall,
odor of chrysanthemums,
timid stations of the cross,
pillars thick, stark.

The man speaks:
Do you see La Virgen?
What I am about to tell you—
I know better—
but you must believe.
I am an educated man,
without superstitions.
Once, when I was a lonely child,
she cried for me,
a large tear from her marble eye
down the length of her clay face.
Don't ask my explaining!—
Her tears were real!

Never, since, has she cried for me.
Never. But I always come to check.
With hope I seek a listener,
tell this story.

Grand Mal

First the siren voice untrackable
sending us swivel-necked in alarm
then outstretched arms toward a place
we cannot go. It will not happen.
This cannot happen to happen
in this place. Haply it does

THIS CLASSROOM RESERVED
for my questions your answers
We come in sit down
look at the pale walls
finger pencils and watches
discourse on the comma

Now galvanic overload unlocks us
from our chairs, sends us to lay her on the floor,
to stand as acolytes to her hushed suffering—
twitch of feet and nibbling lips,
unpaired eyes and moiling fists—
thanks, she is not here.

Then, after light years in our blushing hearts
and seeing she lies quiet on the floor
in a sleep we have to envy, so deep
even her hair asleep, the school nurse beside her,
we go forth Lazaruses into the hall,
out of her storm, saying only with our eyes
that we have seen a miracle, and are risen.

Begging at St. Mark's

Mute light of sacerdotage
after the Adriatic glitter,
carnate pigeons, glassblower's sweat.
Gabrieli's ghost suspended in the dimness,
his dialogs of trumpets and singers
above the altar, great dome
echoing the birth pangs of antiphony;
below, the Second Apostle,
or some donkey as surrogate, resting
inside the jeweled sarcophagus,
the glory of which could feed
a whole starving country.

We've been in line half the day,
the four bronze horses corralled
in scaffolding above us, my mate and I.
He has borne his fever like the pilgrim
he is until he's seen the birthplace
of antiphonal song. Now he sinks
at the foot of a marble pillar.
We're two hours short of our ride
and it's cooler here,
in an airless sort of way,
than outside on the treeless piazza.

I go in search of water but there's none
in this place of baptisteries and communions,
in this shrine threatened with drowning
in the sea. Dry fonts, glass whales
underfoot, schools of mosaics swimming by,
behemoths bellowing out of the psalms—
I'm lost in antiquity. My husband's dry.

Circling to check him again and again,
check his passport, his pulse,
straighten him against the column,
I warn him not to sprawl. He is

too mine this afternoon, and God's,
and perhaps, if I don't watch
more than they, the circling pickpockets'.

Finally, I see the water: retired,
name tags in place, Methodists from Baltimore.
(Are you still there, little wren of a couple,
saying Certainly, proffering an extra cup?)
Be bold in Christ, Saint Mark calls.
So I touch her sleeve, show them my husband
reclined in a Titian slouch, red-faced as marble.

Transubstantiation in a Dixie cup,
Muslims, Buddhists, Hindus and Jews passing by.
Take, Drink, I tell my delirious man.
This is what we get for having faith.

Chant for Those Who Would Sleep

a pantoum

The flickering shall go on all night
    the wind articulating the tree
the tree in fever of moonlight
    the moon enameling me.

The wind articulating the tree
    makes my sleepself a schism.
The moon enameling me
    dreams, forgetful of reason.

My sleeping self a schism
    pewter and patina-crusted spots
lie innocent of reason
    planted and fallow skin plots.

Pewter and patina-crusted spots
    fickle zones of arm and thigh
fallow and tilled skin plots
    harlequin-dash me where I lie.

Fickle zones of arm and thigh
    re-virgined smooth next morning
mottle-splash me as I lie
    in night's wind and tree warning.

Re-virgined smooth next morning
    unpatterned in day and death
in night's wind and tree warning
    I taste the moon's light breath

smoothed by day and death.
    The tree in fever of moonlight
faintly tastes the moon's breath.
    The flickering shall go on all night.

Apotheosis

A hurricane sits like the Cyclops' eye
impaled on the forehead of the Gulf tonight.
It casts itself malevolently about
taking note of the spotter plane,
the radar, the inland escape routes.
We have our provisions: candles, kerosene,
dried beef, transistor. We lay us down
in our cave to rest, the giant
spitting gobbets of wind and rain already.

It is snug in this cave with Polyphemus.
His destruction will be fair:
primeval and classic. If he eats us,
it will be a square meal—no nuclear soup.
The Natural Disaster pamphlet
reads like a souvenir postcard.
We smile in half-sleep. This is why
we did not go straight home to Ithaca.

What If

Like bamboo and monarchs
and salmon, like agave
and the marsupial mouse,
we only made love
one time in our lives—
no headache,
no getting over the flu,
no your mother is coming—
just, This,
This is the time.

We would start in the morning,
spread pallets of silk,
lay out chocolate,
load music: each a choice—
I, the Westminster Boys,
you, all of Stravinsky.

Foreplay until noon,
and then, a hot sun overhead,
we would go until spent,
the last dollar,
high tide and low tide,
interludes,
trips to the kitchen for water,
for fine wine,
so many petits morts
we lose count.

At the very end,
sailing over the moon,
your genitals would explode
like a honeybee's—
my uterus would drop out
like mast on a fir tree.
Small animals would gather round,
eager to take on the strength
of our love.

Bonds

Upon Wanting to Give You the Complete Stories of Flannery O'Connor
for Eleanor

To think of our existence, points on a map,
speck at one end, mite at the other,
squirming down to an awesome blank daily
is not to extend the meaning of despair.
Supposing we two don't matter. To whom?
We got over our fabulous anonymity
one night over coffee. You said it:
that you might raise dogs from now on
and I countered with the profundity
of pouring you more coffee.
We rose, you going to endless abstractions,
I to countable concretions, knowing
only we were alike in some unworded way.

Now some days you stay very neatly
off my mind as I go thinging about.
But often your gold-loving hair appears,
and your green-gathering eyes send me
the jolt and haunt of friendship.
I pause, awed that we are together
at opposite ends of the ribbon on the map.
We talk again, mostly of how we cannot
know what makes us vaguely dizzy.
We are careful about eschatological subjects:
they disquiet us. (We'd rather see than be one.)
We keep to authors, husbands, children,
to comments that sit like clipped hedge
on the periphery of our common presence.
Together or apart, we cannot seem
to say that final thing. The Great Tickle
keeps us clearing our throats.

Thus knowing we can never say what we do know,
very simply, in duet,
from before the tedious business of our births,
until long after we, hating to be unfastidious,
die, let us content ourselves that
we-two-the-fact is that final, overwhelming good
I'd like so much to give you stories about.

We Are Summer
(on being color-analyzed with Judy)

I knew it. There was always
something about us high-toned and full.
Fall? We've done that all right.
Winter? You ski a week each year;
I once rode a ski lift in July.
Spring? Sister, are we sprung?

Yes, summer becomes us.
God, how you let us bloom—
rosy cheeks, rosy lips, rosy eyes:
we're Essence of Rosy.
We're fireflies—lightnin' bugs in Texas.
We glow   now here   now there
sending off signals to mystify all around
even ourselves. We slip the grasp
of our children, blink off on new courses.
Right now we're canoes drifting
on private Waldens, oars at rest,
souls laid back, sunning (true,
a certain harsh glare behind our lids).

And though we're shot through
with summer lightning coming out
of what we thought
was a hot blue cloudless sky,
still, we're cotton, blackberries,
pickles, sunflowers, Johnson grass.
Let's face it: there's something
coming back around in us,
a perennial buzz, a persistent yes.
Summer sister, we're good and ripe.

Afternoon Duty with the Composer

The composer lies dying under the soft green sheet.
She and I have been talking about old times—
fluting "Carnival of the Animals"
and the finale to "A Midsummer Night's Dream"
side by side in the orchestra. She says
her lips are dry now
like when one plays Chaminade's "Concertina"
and a Karl Ellert piece in the same afternoon.
Watching for her to breathe,
I think of her notes like unmarked graves
on pages at home in a small cabinet.
She repeats herself: "He was better on strings
on strings." I check the catheter—
eighth notes drift to the plastic bag.
a fermata or two, a clef sign.
She asks for a drink.
Her hair crescendos on the pillow.
I fill the syringe and
her tiny embouchure closes on the plastic tip
(no silver tone hole today).
I ask if she is tired of holding hands.
She strains, *"No. No. Continuoso!"*
She is surprised to know
we have been friends sixteen years.
Today I do not hesitate
to write a poem about a sick friend.
At times there are no other poems.
We are alone in this world of afternoon.
We don't have our flutes.
We aren't exchanging tricky fingerings,
but we are playing the best duet,
the one not possible before.

The Specified Donor
for Rob

Mahogany and henna, the sack above my head
like a flask of vintage wine
brings memory of you, hope for me.

At two I doze, despite the plastic
noise around
then start to a mockingbird's song.

Saturdays you prowl the sanctuary
field glasses trained
for groove-billed ani or loggerhead shrike.

Once we shuttled a question between us
for several weeks:
What is a group of hawks called?

Solving the riddle with "kettle"
we've moved on
spiralling in the thermals, with "life"

a vague answer to the new question
unspeakably perched
on the foot of my bed tonight.

Toward dawn I begin on the hospital plan:
L's and H's of floors,
vents, elevators, stresses, exits

while your blueprints for seven projects
hang like clean laundry
on their rack in your office cross-town.

Now the weak light shows rain
against the sealed glass
as uneven and luxuriant as the blood inversely

obeys its precious calibrated drip
on the alchemist's command—
platelets, albumin, plasma descending

like charms. The least I can do
is pray the clouds
harmless to you, gone fishing in Mexico

first giving this tagged present,
premier valentine
with your name in bold marker.

The power surge leaves me with fever,
your blood sending
my blood into a feeding frenzy.

At dawn they disarm us abruptly,
take away our connections,
I move out of mummified pose,

out of the figure imprinted on the sheet,
find I have not for myself
held a wake but a vigil.

The doctor comes, sees you already
teased into my nails.
Now I doze, first sending you

deep in the *campo*, beside the lake
of giant bass
a pink smile, my new and only brother.

Sistering

I. Just a theory

A friendship steady as a star:
that's the cliché we began with,
like Venus planted and winking
dependably.
　　　　You are gone now,
turned back to your family:
husband and three children.
There is no room for me, you said,
because it wasn't right,
I deserved more than letters
from the end of your day.
Therefore, you don't write at all.

Your Christmas card (the first I knew
from two years past of you:
children and spouse are happy,
as well as dog) comes like a comet
trailing flashed-out times,
saying friendship is event,
not condition,
saying if we ever thought us
star-crossed sisters,
know you had moved on
to other galaxies.

II. A delicate question

But wasn't I afraid of my doctor,
after seeing her and the woman she lived with
in the grocery store? I mean, couldn't she
violate me or be loving me, or wanting me,
or whatever one woman could do to another
during a pelvic?

I count them, 18 male doctors over the years.

I think a little about each.
C'mon, I say,
No, I am not afraid.

III. Between wolf and wombat

You are closer than household tips,
"girlfriend," "lady friend" or "gal."
The ad for the new chapbook says
send them poems on Friendship, like
"beer-buddies, war-buddies and
fellow workers." Disqualified,
you and I snicker.
"Sister worker" won't quit sounding
like a shout from a tent revival.
Coffee and trouble mix as well as
beer and pretzels.

I will risk "hysteria" with you.
Also "no sense of humor"
and being a "case of nerves."
In the dictionary before "woman"
comes "wolf." After "woman" come
"womanhood, womanish, womanize,
womankind, womanly, woman suffrage, womb."

Then there's "wombat."

My sister, somewhere between
wolf and wombat we are.
But far from endangered.
Far from extinct.

IV. Soft shoe and whistling with my mother-in-law

Today I put away your garters, scarves, sachet
you never thought yourself good enough to use.
Folding up your dresses, airy and full of flowers,
took a long time, a certain quaintness in it all.
You left a tissue in each pocket, often a grocery list,

phone number. There were dresses you intended to wear,
some you overwore, favorites ready like anxious puppies.
I keep myself reasonable, at high tide all day
not to spoil the job.

Into eight boxes I have put the round and malleable you,
as Picasso might send his tender blue woman on the shore
up the harsh stairs of Avignon, or as the difference
in your breasts when you would lie down,
the real one heading for comfort beside your silky inner arm,
the other, fashioned of plastic,
stubborn as a mountain over the mass of scars.
(I took your prosthesis with your burial clothes,
then was sorry to see it stiff and ridiculous on your chest
like a separate casket for your given-out heart.)

For three weeks I have carried you in a bundle in my head.
Tonight your wavy gray hair, green eyes are an aquarium
among the periwinkles, roses, fleurs-de-lis of your dresses.
I lie down in the boxes that will be taken tomorrow,
smell the faint odor meaning you,
love you out of my generation, as my sister.
I ask for some strength you let go of,
your 70 years to take me places I have not been.
You call to me over the powder dish, the brooches,
saying a woman's life is worth dying for,
saying never mind the stiff breast we could not fix,
saying it lies pinned to you now like a medal of honor.

Riddle in Two Voices

Mother, in the world you made for two sisters,
blackberries stained; ice cream, like a cloud,
could be eaten with a spoon, clean and nice.
Respectability was the cliff our toes curled over
when we practiced our backyard trapeze act,
readied ourselves for the circus life—acrobatic girls,
matching floozies, circus queens—We'd show you!
Pretty is would not be pretty does.

Girls, oh my little blackberry desserts, skinny ones,
so full of gritty seeds, I see you far away today,
mere clouds and voices above the cliff of my mothering.
I thought to keep you safe from the whir and click
of circus carnie rides, sew you to me
with a needle of love I finally couldn't thread,
lick my fingers over and over to set the knot.
A stitch in time saves nine? Not even two.

Sisters, in the Pool

Twilight and the sun has shrunk to a scarlet ball
between the Rose of Sharon and the oak,
exactly the same as when we were girls.
Someone says, "You can tell it's August by the way
the sun just hangs there on the gray air."
It is the only thing certain in our lives right now
—the rest unclear: our parents' bodies and minds,
what to do, what not, our children,
their fortunes, moves, health, marriages.
You wear a gauzy bath cap
over your delicate blonde wedge,
not a bubbly rubber cap but headgear
fit for Juliet on a balcony.
You raise your arms high, out of the water,
and their undersides glow pure and white
in the evening light. (Would mine look the same?)
We gossip the family secrets, rush to the side, laughing,
when the neighbors' pot smoke jumps the fence.

What is there to do but go on—imperfect decisions,
resolutions, substitute dreams, and fear—
all that which is less simple than the silky undersides
of middle-aged arms, Shakespearean bath caps,
the sun on fire with its dying?

Mother,

       when I try to say you,
you change in my mouth to a myth
told beside a fire to children
lest they forget who they are.

Mother, when I try to say you,
I don't know where you end,
protozoan dividing in slow motion
down ages of fission.

I didn't know I was you until I was thirteen.
A long civil war ensued.
We're still repatriating each other.

Mother, when I try to say you,
you become a hot torch
I'm running with, never,
never going out my whole life's running.

Father,

there is a while now when you and I
may walk as friends within our days,
for I am not the child demanding praise
nor you the old man ambitious to die.
We are suspended in the double why
of child and father. Gone the phase
of boosting me to your shoulder in a craze
of paternity. Not yet for you I cry.
This remembering, let us reason
that words of weather and such talk
will rob us of discovering the other
who is most like ourselves. In this season
brief with honesty, let's take a walk,
say only words which hearten one another.

Sixty-seventh Anniversary

Their love runs deep and down.
Scowls, words pitched like pond stones,
blaming silences all mitigated

by love: loud goodnight smacks,
caresses designed to steady,
parade of coffee, roll call of dead friends.

He says it's good he doesn't own a gun.
She says she won't last 'til her birthday.
Putting on their shoes takes all morning.

"Go on now," she says, prodding him
when he sticks like a cat in the doorway,
leftover control twitching in his face.

"Your mother doesn't have any idea
at all what's become of her purse," he rats.
"I have to watch her constantly."

They keep switching canes, like relay runners.
"Why not mark them?" a daughter tries.
"Heavens, no!" they bawl in unison.

"Nothing like that..." the old woman starts,
"...makes the slightest bit of difference," he finishes.

Getting in Touch with Mother

With no snappy top, spigot, or pump,
her Jergens bottle, wide-mouthed, glass-hipped,
might be too generous at her tip and shake,
give her far more lotion than she
could possibly be beautiful in,
even counting neck and elbows.
She'd bid me, stuck in the doorway,
"Come. Give me your hands."

I'd spring forward, lay palms to hers,
thrilled at this invitation to high fives.
Then she'd coat me with her excess,
first slathering on the glamour milk,
now feeling of my hands like fine fabrics,
now massaging, squeezing,
me knowing to stay utterly limp,
and finally, trolling each finger
as my giggles rose no-holds-barred
from this daring grown-up wetness.

Our lovely handwrestling complete,
and fresh out of her emergency,
all almond-scented and smooth
I'd stand alone again.

Certainty

Before this second life, he knew everything,
especially what heaven was like,
and earned his living telling folks what pleasure
dying was, his time with daughters measured
out in yardsticks of piety, responsibility, and care.
The earthly coulds were under wraps of shoulds.

Sex didn't exist, except embarrassment of his:
two daughters there as the nose on his face.
At this remove, I know his supper table commands
for what they were: fear. That day some
grieving mother had poured out to him the news
of her unmarried pregnant daughter.

First, observation:
"These blackbirds here at my feeder
come several times a day to peck peck peck."
Then, apology:
"Sorry you see me like this.
I know enough to know I don't know anything."
And finally, declaration:
"I love you so very very"
and his eyes rinse out his heart.

He gave me watches for birthdays—
"Take care of it—especially in the rain;
Don't overwind; no dropping, no whacking"
They lie in my jewelry box, time scrambled.

Now, if there's time, he tells me
he doesn't have the foggiest idea
what heaven is like. He says he's ready,
really ready. The nights are every one too long.

Days, his watch is his best friend:

"They're bringing my pills."
"It's time for the food."
"They come for the clothes in 25 minutes."

With wool socks I brought last time,
he's built a threshold under his door,
Over these we step each time we enter.
"This time of year it's crickets, crickets
the world over, crickets by the buckets."
He smiles, the rhyme pleasing
some old elegant poetry-quoting place.

He consults his watch.
"One thing's for sure, honey:
you better go before they lock the door."

Expedition

Falling to bed together
we are not independent explorers:
you plundering my cache
I carving initials on your monolith
you knotting a ropeway after dark
I honing my ice ax softly.

Rather. We shod each other,
enumerate supplies,
map our third world—the high country
of volcanoes and daisies,
alps with flying buttresses
of rainbows,
aurora borealis
of our northern kingdoms.

When we are home again,
neither speaks of conquering,
of being first to raise the flag
shouting down soundless words
to the other waiting below
in the heavenly cold
of the sub-station.
We descend
hand in hand,
the secrets of the view
gritty in our eyes,
the salt of the wind
on our tongues,
the music of suns
strolling our brains.

Basic Difference

Finding her gown
and making sure
(most profound!)
the appliqued flowers
faced front,
unsecuring the door,
noticing that time
had gone by quite fast
so now the night
was too short
for tomorrow's tasks,
wondering if any child
was pitching nightmare
or nosebleed,
pulling open the shade
for a little more air,
she turned around to see that,
for the love of her,
he had gone to sleep.

I Cut Open a Papaya/ My Husband Reads His UFO Journal

Seven months we have waited, looking into the garden
as this fruit becomes a world, at first a hard green egg,
then so slight a blush, we argue with our vision,
rely on yesterday's color, and in the final month,
wonder if it's deep gold or the sunset's bounce;
chant against the possum shinnying up the trunk,
the wasp finding entry, the grackle's stony stare.

Quince, apricot, and finally, marigold: it's time.
"I'm going to pick it," my husband says after supper,
a householder's evening chore more interesting than dishes.
He bolts out the door, twists the three-pound ellipsoid free.
I watch from the window.

Now he sits in a room nearby, reading of grays, abductees.
I split the papaya with my sharpest knife,
the sound like my water breaking with our first child.
A galaxy of black planets rushes to the light,
a hundred or two shining ova with a flurry
of green impatient sprouts. I scoop the seeds in reverence,
save them on a plate. He wants to dry and plant them,
plant them all, row upon row. Peeling,
I slice a wedge, bite the gold, lean to the sink,
the musky flesh in my mouth after all these months.
I take a taste to him.

In another dimension, by lamplight, he raises his head,
opens his mouth. He samples, blinks up at me
from inner space. Yes, he agrees, this melon planet
is unexplainable—from stick, sunlight, water, grace.
Back in the kitchen, I make conserve, stirring the pot
of saffron: papaya, pineapple, sugar, lemon.
I'm humming thanks to the woman far away
who shared this recipe; I'm barely contained

by the row of glittering jars with pretty labels.
I'm happy.

"Hmmm." I hear him sigh and shift,
likely off to the hunt, pursuing cigar-shaped airships,
enemies with slanted eyes, patterns in wheat.
Suddenly he's leaning in the doorway.
"Listen to this," and he reads from outer space.
I stand listening, sucking my sticky fingers,
our marriage hovering, listening, marking us.

Sharing the House

Dealing in Futures

The sonogram snows, then straightens
to a quarter-pie of glacial bed,
conglomerate tumbling, glowing debris.
Now a shape too sharp for chance appears,
a form swimming through glitter.
Puffy eyes, blunt nose, no chin.
It gives a charming marmot smile.

The doctor calibrates in flowers,
stop-actioning with tiny asterisks
to measure side to side, front to back.
The femur shines like a sunken ingot,
receives the blessed centimeters;
the brain lobes are twins, thank God,
and sit distinct in reason, art.

We're cool, dispassionate until we see
this spirit-life experiments with agendas:
an astronaut afloat in cabin fever,
harpist practicing arpeggios,
cyclist pedalling watery meters
on a bike not yet imagined.

While we strive to find (eyes watering
from stares or seeing our future fleshed)
a boy? a girl?—oblivious to voyeurism,
it bends to play with feet, check toes.
And then insistently declining our offer
to know its sex, it settles to taste a thumb,
and for this one last time a mystery,
to moon us.

You ask me to describe the pain at your birth

Trains run on schedule through the belly
Mountains cry
Tigers pace and glare
A delicious fever comes for lunch

One is trying to catch the train
comfort the mountains
make friends with beasts
find a suitable chair for the fever

One is trying to stay on the narrow gauge
One is undecided about mountain train rides
One dreams briefly of the red mouths of animals
One notices the fever circling the edge of light

The tunnel rushes forward
The mountains collapse
The tigers burst their cages
The fever tames, becomes you.

Chewing

"Want me to feed you?" he wonders
after he's cut the meat.

"Sure," I say and ease upright
on the fresh surgical star.
His plane is leaving in two hours.
He's stayed just long enough
to cheer the baby out of hiding,
ill at ease with people into sex,
having babies, even his own daughter.

I begin to chew, each bite of supper
paying like a nub of peyote—

connections: a child fed by a father
because she has had his grandchild,
bite after bite, the genealogies
called to supper, I chewing backward
to my father, he feeding forward to my child.

food chains: home in books
where sun pours down from the top
of pages with crowded pasture,
ant, hawk, mouse, and snake,
the cow at work on her alfalfa.

feasting: Last Supper, 4th Floor Maternity,
my father not unsaintly
offering me the bread of life,
I eating that I might be filled,
salvation in postpartum.

The tray is taken. He kisses, goes.
I lie back, rest, hear his plane
as the nurse wings in with my child.

Of fathers feeding their grown daughters,

of those same daughters feeding their newborns,
I tell my son. He learns with pitiful squall
the what and where of food. When he finally sucks,
I laugh, the laughter rising in me
for the chewed meat, the fresh milk,
the grandfather circling up and over
like a night hawk in the evening sky.

Animal/Vegetable/Mineral/Childkeeper

Child, you are small; your presence great.
Is this fate or miracle?
My life is getting late.

Shading you like redwood, I have to wait
an age for you to grow before I fall.
Child, you are small; your presence great.

The stone monument I am endures your prate
like Lot's wife, salty and dull.
My life is getting late.

I multiply, rabbits of melted chocolate
running the maze of your drool.
Child, you are small; your presence great.

You bring me afternoons to create
you out of; time is the cruelest tool.
My life is getting late.

Riddle me this: How can I support the weight
of you at play inside my skull?
Child, you are small; your presence great.
My life is getting late.

Lady Tiresias

Why do you bring me your dreams,
bear them in like breakfast to my bed,
your eyes bright for telling,
holding me there until each
diamonded monster, licorice piece,
red motorcycle spill on me
who asks nothing but to waken gently?

I hide behind a yawn.
I blink and say Really?
You pause at the foot
of some midnight cliff,
purple paint on your hands.
You insist a dog comforts you
in Spanish.

The whole thing's out.
Now you sleep an early-morning
hard and dreamless bit
against my arm
like a stone-clinging snail.
Later you will skip to your day
clean and unharmed. And I?
I'll set off for the marketplace,
mind full of bird entrails
and strange cries overhead
for what's in store for you.

To a boy who lost his first tooth today

Goodnight, fresh jack-o'-lantern.
I pry open your fist to take the pebble
washed up on the narrowing shore
of your smallness today.

I lean to kiss you—careful as a mosquito—
and pay you a dime to stay little,
believe in me.
　　　But you are six and bony.
What if your knees, nose, wrist bones
are all teeth working to the surface?

Okay, I'm going, snaggletooth.
Grant me the quiet closing of your door.
This game we play is serious.
I scuttle down the hall to hide
your appleseed among my jewels.
The next move is yours.

Nothing on earth can stop your bones
from stretching in the dark,
making you tall enough some day
to find among my high-placed necklaces
this fragile pearl you lost.
You will turn it over and over
in your hand and study my message:

The trust of a child has no roots.
Forgive me a kernel's worth.
Take this talisman for your knowing.

Crack of Dawn

I found you
one morning
awake too early,
coiled in your covers
against the chill,
your drawing tablet,
a pencil, the "L"
of the encyclopedia.

My son, did anyone
ever tell you
eight year olds
in America
do not sketch
from Leonardo
on cold mornings?
No one has given you
instructions for shaping
the aquiline nose,
shading the *sfumato*.

You are
a sketchbook intact,
a flying machine,
a Milanese horse,
a Florentine sundial.

You are the reason
behind my enigmatic smile.

Doing What Comes Naturally

Nature is usually wrong.
James Whistler

We are told that hens, given ducklings to rear,
will pick at the adopteds' webbed feet
until that stretchy business is cleared.
Also that geese have been known
to lead orphaned chicks into the water
for a swimming lesson.

As innocently begin the visits to the orthodontist
to make piano keyboards of our darlings' mouths,
trips to the oculist to be sure the kids see
the world exactly as God does.

Babies are tricks. They aren't called
lambkin, pet, chickabiddy for nothing.

So when knees go bony, middles thick,
when shoulders round
and pimples make the cheeks rosy,

when nosebleeds and dandruff
interfere with perfection,

cracked knuckles and bitten nails
supplant the sweet thumb,

when one day you realize
Uncle Alonzo's nose has sprouted
like a mushroom on your teen's face,

that your daughter has gotten her father's bosom
and your son, his mother's double-A feet: remember
the Ugly Duckling was only a fairy tale
without a surrogate mom

and Mother Goose was no good at anything
but making rhymes.

99

Lies, You Wish

At least the tooth was in hand.
You could play games with it.
But the voice is no toy.
It's a bullfrog
grafted for keeps
on that sweet neuter throat.
It's a rodeo horse bucking
soprano or bass laughter.

There are other sinister signs:
dirty top lip
(you'd hoped it was newspaper print),
Adam's apple deliberately
hunchbacking.

Inanimate objects conspire as well:
chairs beg to be kicked.
Tables scrunch down.
Doors slam on privacy.
Corners, ceilings, floor tiles
make themselves more interesting
to look at than you.

One morning a stranger sits before you,
silently forking his egg: he has bad news.
Seems your child jumped ship in the night.

A changeling swims in your eyes.
From now on, you must invent
the relationship.

Braving the Atlantic

One of these days
I am going to make sense
of your junk-filled room,
roll out generations
of Puritan godliness
on you to show
you have been wrong,
have strayed from the heritage,
can never be happy in a mess.

This could hurt.
That's why I keep stalling,
wondering if your room is a mirage—
if the Mayflower just
thought it landed.

Instance of Continuum

Seventeen. To Italy. Every long leg-tickling apron string
clipped from your cut-offs yesterday as you packed.
"A chain," I said as we drove you to the airport,
"your luggage key needs a chain," but already
you were crooning half to your brothers, half yourself,
"Look at that!" as the sun came rolling through
squadrons of morning clouds.

      Then, you gone to it,
 plunged into the Sunday sky as final as you plunged
from me wailing at birth. Yet the umbilical cord trails
after you—unloops, spins out longer and longer
flaying the stratosphere, guywire angling from the ground,
holding.

      When you were three,
your balloon floated over the backyard fence
for a high surveillance of the subdivision.
You screamed the scream of a primal creature who knows
only that it hurts, and flung yourself to the grass.
Later on my lap, resigned to the heavenly ascension,
you learned to say, "Some things don't last forever,"
and for years afterward used the maxim
coming to grips with change.

      Today you are gone,
 freefloating astronaut giddy with weightlessness,
impatiently training the cord behind you, behind you,
while I, the heavy, strain hand over raw hand in a game
of tug-of-war gone serious, a fisherman forgetting
the catch out of need to save his gear.

But this thing stays, two-ended,
despite all our efforts to connect or disconnect,
silent principle awaiting the birth of Pythagoras,
calculated distance to an undiscovered star
as even your ticket, flying you now to Italy

waits to loop you home again,

as even the childhood truth you needed:
    "Some things don't last forever"
can never bisect this line between us.

My Other 499,997 Children

At birth the female ovaries contain
about 500,000 egg cells.
                    biological fact

What kind of joke it was
packing your mother with
five-hundred-thousand potential children,
half—squirming like maggots in the left side,
the same snarled as a golf ball's inside on the right,
I'll never understand.

It must be something on the same principle
as the beehive selecting a larval queen to feed,
or a hundred acres of wildflowers
belly-laughing the sky.

Children three, I want to teach you your randomness.
You are chancy as smears,
common as brick in a skyscraper.

Your odds are laughable, micronomic.

Think it over. I could tell you
you are special to me, that I was thinking
only of you when I conceived.

I'd rather you contemplate the high stakes,
the ridiculous behavior of the universe,
know your own mind-boggling appearance
as miracle outside my saying so.

I'd rather you stand under a swarm of stars
on a billion grains of sand
and claim yourself.

Nature Lesson

Having swarmed the picnic tables,
having deposited our guano at rest areas,
here we are, of the genus *familias vacationas*
perched in the amphitheatre
to see the bats swarm out of Carlsbad at sunset.
        There will be a high squealing sound,
          a rush of wings. The sky will blacken.
We sit, not knowing how to wait for a natural wonder.

The moment approaches.
A few avant-garde black whirs—we are thrilled—
Get quiet!—a few more, and more, then. . .
the rain counter-attacking in big Vampire splotches,
zapping every precious bat back down that dark hole,
carrying the message: not tonight.

We sit on, asking if bats ever change their minds
in a light sprinkle, just a shower.
We gather bits of the stormy dusk with our eyes
and make them flap, shriek,
anything to show us we're having a good time
on our summer vacation.

Grown

I am borrowing shirts
they have burst from as men,
stepping into jeans I say
I will only paint in,
pulling on their sweaters for walks,
sleeping in their better wool socks.

Once they teased me with cicada shells
gathered from trunks of mesquite
outside their windows. Thorax split,
vacant eyes bulging, exoskeletons
appeared on my pillow at bedtime,
sang in my hair at restaurants.

Today, warm in their cast-offs,
I await the coming of summer,
listen for voices high-pitched,
the call to new seasons.

Sharing the House

Blessings on your body
which is my body
and on my body
which is yours.

Blessings on this mutual animal
of the third world,
our shared cells,
and on all future knowing of it
past the slow erosions
of age and separation.

Blessings on the simpleness
of owning each other,
of letting each other go,
of the stubborn, blind meaning
and second nature
and the inborn touching.

Blessings on this love that runs
deep into the earth
and springs up as grass
and small animals,
that sets out on the long journey
to the stars
and meets us
rising in our deaths,
telling us
it returns
to declare the bond
to new mothers, new sons.

Nearly Off the Map

I come to bed a while after you
in this old farmhouse
after checking the mousetraps
and children (an extra blanket
heaved down from a closet
for a scrunched-up one who smiled
when it fanned his hair).
There is a puppy on the porch
and a pair of lizards
under the papers on my desk.

I make myself as much like you
as you, and am not wrong in it:
I have on your other pajamas.
In sleep you take my cold hand,
fold it into your shirt.
My cold feet become your soles.

When I am warm, you release me
as though I signal in your dream.
I roll away to listen to the rain
begin to tap the orchard leaves,
the gathering wind choose a ripe fruit.

My poems stir—the lizards mating,
biting necks, him into her,
sex duty for this house tonight.

Through spacious dark
the planet slings our bed.

Midcourse

Shopping for Time

The future is the present—only later.
                    bathroom wall
                    Cody's Books, Berkeley

We are tomorrow's past!
                    senior class slogan, 1992

Standing flat-arch still
outside the storefront
I note the reflected I
is not the future,
the hope of tomorrow,
or what-lies-ahead.

This face is cold sober,
cash on the barrelhead,
no credit or lay-away,
a big deposit, no return,
expiration date: sundown.
Shift the load, it says.
You have a while before home.

Over in the Produce Department
(fresh from an article on estrogen)

I am reaching for the quiet
ovarian kohlrabi when,
sudden as a dragon's tongue,
the sprinkler system begins,
startling me back to estrogen
delivered from little kohlrabis
in our opposing sides each month.

So which is this, this water
I dry off my arm:
for greener pastures,
or to put out the fire?

Touring a Well-seasoned Woman

Notice the brow
moves toward translucence,
that the eyes telegraph more, oh
much more now that they have
their radiating lines.

See how the light
plays warm on the cheek,
cool in the cliffside of the neck.

On your right is one breast,
on your left, the other.
These have a history of stories:
sighing babes and oblivious lovers.

Now we come to the belly,
all Greek, convexed in marble.
The hips, we see,
are posing for Rubens.

You will observe how the thighs
have stepped delicately
out of their hair,
how the calves stay faithfully
curved on the road
to their twin intentions,

how the feet tell all time and tide.

The Make-up Poem

"There is a garden in her face"
                 Thomas Campion
                 1567-1620

Yes, it is
frivolous
expensive
time-consuming
artificial
dangerous
and unworthy.

Yes, it mimes
the posterior
sexual colorations
of the adult
male mandrill.

Yes, the number
of products
pawned off
on women,
with "rev-"
"-some"
and "-ique"
in their names
is indeed
scandalous.

No, a woman's face
can't need
toner, blusher,
liner, smudger,
powder, cover,
enhancer—
plus base,
lotion, stick,

114

and rouge
all at once.

And yes, I shall wear it.
For: The names are beautiful.
This is closet art.
Men without are not better
than women with.
Nature loves a color display.
Clowns and mimes are magic.

A Night School Lit Student Fulfills her 500-Word Essay by Channeling Julia, on the Juices in her Life

Whenas in silks my Julia goes,
Then, then (methinks) how sweetly flows
That liquefaction of her clothes.
            Robert Herrick
            1591-1674

Funny you should notice, Robert Herrick,
that liquefaction of my clothes.
Maybe so, wearing liquids,
but the truth is
anything wet is what we
women are tending to.

Womenfolk, don't ever let yourself
be convinced it's only the fire
you were left to tend. Hunh-unh.
What's hot goes out.

The first liquefaction, of course,
is our blood,
our tend-yourself monthlies
assigned us by the moon.
Then there may be a spate
of bright drops like Morse code,
undercover messages,
perhaps-children,
until one finally makes it.

There's where women
get into that second generational
mop-up and the divine right
of being in charge of milk.
Milk is a major juice
and it's the one originally
assigned to women

so I have no complaints about it
particularly when my babies
were swilling it like little pigs,
all full of sighs and looking up
in that break-your-heart trusting way,
and later,
kicking and pushing and kneading
like they were one of ten in a litter
of German Shepherds.
Nope, milk is the original juice
and from there all these other assignments.
Unless of course, you go way back
and talk about Eve and juice.

"I sure like kumquat jelly," Adam said.
"Same here," said the snake.
And there Eve was, clicking the food processor
on-off, good-evil, on-off, good-evil
until she got a batch.
She added sugar and a little pectin
but when you look at World History charts,
you can see what a lot of good that did.

Speaking of time lines,
we can go on with our own,
speaking after the juice of milk
of blood again, this time nosebleeds
(the best one I ever had resulted
from an afternoon of heavy petting
and had to be stopped by a nurse
in the neighborhood)

and dripping knees
from skateboard miscalculations
and then body-length scrapings
where a teenager has gone
down the road on his motorbike
using himself as a spare tire.
Now there's juice like a scraped turnip.
I do not want to talk about scalp wounds

(there is just too much to clean up there)
much less gunshot juice
you see women hunched over on the news
trying to do something about.

The other juices women have been assigned
have a Relative Humidity Factor—
they all have to do with relatives.
First category you've got your wet sheets.
They are caused by three reasons:
        There's love,
        There's sleep,
        There's trouble
spilling out, competing with each other
for why the sheets have to be washed.
I read a book once by one John Updike
where the main fornicators
did it in the laundry room
on a pile of already-dirty sheets
and I thought that was about
the sanest thing I'd ever heard
of an author letting his characters do.

The way I see it,
for every I-love-you and stuff in the world,
a woman will have a sheet to wash.
Nobody's going to stand up and say it,
mainly because the men crawl out
and go make money or go home
so they never think of the sheets
when they write the books.

And when one of these women writes
a romance book, she doesn't want to put
at the end of Chapter Two, after
the first lovemaking scene,
that Brandy Nicole had to flail about
taking the sheets off the bed
after Trey had gone and taken
all his steely hardness,

and that she had to trudge
to the laundry room with them,
and then get fresh ones
and flap and spread them,
walking back and forth around the bed. No.

So she doesn't say it,
so young people reading how love is to be made
don't think at all about this part,

and then when a female young person
gets into the game, she wonders,
all by her lone self in the whole wide world,
why she never knew that
changing the sheets
was all there was to afterplay.

Well, that's just humidity in love.
Now humidity, or liquidity,
or liquefaction as Robert liked to call it,
in sleep is another province of woman's role
as Tender-of-Juices.
And that is two ways:

1) children whose pee is frightened out of them
by booger bears, or as they said
once on TV, something in their neuron dreams
that fails to fire in the bladder
causing them to be totally un-neat
and

2) male children who are practicing
Wet Sheets in Love for later on.

And I would not say a woman is guiltless
in wet sheets herself. She is capable of
making her own.
Like way later on, after she's tended
children's wet beds for various reasons
and her love's bed for one reason,

she's so addicted to wet sheets she dreams
up a way to get her own, like night sweats.
Like waking up wringing wet and looking to see
a reasonable facsimile of herself
where she has just a moment ago been dreaming,
that she's playing Angels in the Snow
by new rules,
so she has to get up and mop her hairline
and find a new gown
and sleep on a towel the rest of the night
because her side of the bed is so wet.
And in the morning her hair looks like
a listing shrimp boat.

Well, the one final major category of liquefaction
that women are in charge of is tears.
These can come any time, any place.
So a woman must go forth with her basic tool—
a tissue in her pocket.
Show me a woman without a tissue in her pocket
and I'll show you a woman marooned on an island
in the Pacific, between hers, and her kids'
and their friends' and her sisters' tears.

And if someone gets sad after lights out, then
Bang! there's that sheet to wash again next morning
because of the big dried Salt Lake
someone has deposited there in all his/her
gypped, jaded, and jingo feelings.
Which is here probably just as good a place as any
to say that a sub-category of tears liquid
is snot, though, with that,
we would have to include the common cold,
which of course women are in charge of.

And moving on down, from the eyes and nose,
there is spit, which we are also in charge of.
My grandbaby loves it when I dab his drool.
He wants that tissue over and over,
two dozen times if I'll do it,

and he'll even blow fresh glommy bubbles if I quit,
just to prompt me for another round of dabbings.

And my mother, in the rest home,
needs a little help too controlling this category
because something is coming all undone in her jaws
and glands, and although she doesn't talk any more,
I think of her little ropes of spit as liquid words
that are trying to get out of her any way they can.
Maybe she is trying to say that she kept pretty busy
with juices all her life too.

In conclusion, the way I see it, Robert Herrick, is this:
(and please, Professor, don't grade me off for this)

If the earth is three-fourths covered with water
and our bodies are two-thirds water, and
women are a little more than half the world's folk,
shouldn't some of this liquefaction be leaking over
to the men's side?

Diana the Huntress Goes for her Mammogram

She had to leave her deer
in the underground parking,
check her bow at the door.
Her turn came before she could
put the touch on a woman in labor
or advise a virgin or two.
How did she want to pay? Pay?
Her father had influence.
She donned her gown right over left
and left over nothing.
After they took off her armband,
they asked the date of her period.
She said Pre-history to Golden Age.
The plexiglass flattened
her breast like a discus.
"Ouch!" she said in Greek.
"Hold your breath, miss."
The plexiglass squeezed her
sideways into tableau.
"Ouch!" she tried it in Latin.
"I'm not from Egypt."
"Hold your breath, miss."
Finished, Lady Wild Things
dropped her toga to one shoulder,
fetched her bow and quiver,
exited in long strides.
Her little dog waited
by the elevator.

Headache

A stone demands birth, Zeus-style.
One eye makes a lunch of itself.
A lobotomy? Sure.
Hair complains of crookedness
in high places. It's rush hour
in the veins, a brownout
north of the city.

Buy futures in sewage. For tears,
bring on Victoria Falls.
The wall is cooler than the bed.
The floor is lower than the chair.
Did my parents sin?
What will I think with hereafter?

Scars

As children we found them useful,
ever available for quiet distraction
through the long sermons and lessons:
a white worm on a finger from a knife,
a ridge in the chin checked for sensation,
bars of a furnace grate amusing an arm.
We told our stories of them,
fondled them with love and pride.
They were the edges we lived on.

We did not know each had a mate,
a future double waiting skip-stitched
or red-mounded or fine white-seamed,
waiting for the soul,
fate making a list,
checking it twice.

Menopause Ain't No Tunnel of Love

"Have you 'been through' menopause?" everyone asks you,
including your sister, the insurance man, tele-strangers,
like you might have taken the vacation of a lifetime
through an eighth wonder of the world, a Disneyworld fun ride
burrowed through a mountain, and come out on the other side
laughing and unscathed. "Been through?" you say,
like the words were brand new.
"Is that anything like the valley of the shadow of death?"
They don't seem to know.
"Been through?" You just read somewhere
it might take ten years to get through menopause.
Maybe the best ten years of your life? Oh, come on...
Suck up! Don't be a wimp! Stiff-arm it!
Still...you can't help but remember the graffiti
on your dream bathroom wall:
"Menopause ain't no tunnel of love"
and another line beneath, answering:
"It's more like the English Channel Chunnel."

So what happens when you first start in?
You still see the light, it's not so dim.
You're only 47 and the first you've heard
that you're in it is when your doctor
writes under "diagnosis" on your check-up:
"pre-menopausal."
Well—but—you keep your hair sun-streaked,
you're doing step aerobics;
you're wearing jeans and sneaks;
you're lo-cal and fat-free
and crunching Tums,
Hogwash on menopause, you say,
I don't know what they mean.

And yet...and yet...
Something's going on in your chin and jaw
when you look at yourself in the mirror—
it's your grandmother come to call.
Suddenly they begin to have menopause features on TV,
and pieces in the newspaper on estrogen,

and the lead articles in magazines change from
"How to be Better in Bed" to
"Surviving Midlife Crises."

Suddenly, moisturizer seems
like a very good and natural product,
and if you can only hold your shoulders back,
and your stomach in, and your head up,
and walk three miles every morning,
and keep having your period
(even though it's been a bit wimpy lately)
there's no way you're
even going to think about the big M.

Then, one night, you dream
you're in front of an oven
only it's not bread that's baking, it's you!
And you wake up and say, "Ha,ha, just kidding"
except there's another you,
a wet one, on the sheet beneath you,
a variation of "Angels in the Snow",
except this ring of wet hair around your face
is no halo. So you get up gamely and dry off
and change your gown and go back to bed
to ponder this new kind of wet dream.
Then you notice that your husband
is whistling softly beside you
and recall that he hasn't whistled at you lately,
and you count the dogs barking in the neighborhood,
and a little later you hear the papers slapping the driveways,
and you move on to committee assignments and grocery lists
and from there to sick friends and difficult relatives
and then to deadly viruses and airplane crashes,
and right on out to world hunger and warring nations
and nuclear fission pirates, and Adolf and Omar and Saddam.
Then the alarm rings.

Maybe you'll go out to the mall today
and maybe stop in at Waldenbooks
and maybe drop over to the Health and Fitness section,
and maybe, just maybe
get that Gail Sheehy book on menopause.

And all of a sudden it's dark in the tunnel
and the sign says,
>TURN ON YOUR LIGHTS;
>YOU ARE IN PERI-MENOPAUSE.

And you do obediently, and keep on going,
deeper and deeper, whistling as you go.
It's interesting terrain, you tell yourself,
self-reliant as you are at 51,
a modern woman doing her thing:
then you catch a resemblance of yourself in the landscape:
ever-so-subtle erosion of lips,
elbows metamorphosing (your grandchild
calls them "rumply"), buns turning sedimentary.
Suddenly there's a big red light: "Trouble Up Ahead."
You slow down, check your seat belt:
>Your womb is bleeding buckets
>but the rest of you is dry.
>Your OB-Gyn is yawning,
>asking why it is you cry.
>(You cry some more the day he says
>his mother, as well as you,
>has aches and pains at 52.)
>Your headaches are most interesting,
>you lose your grocery list,
>Your doctor says it's hormones
>now you miss. But not to worry,
>you'll be dandy—wait 'n see
>with hormone replacement therapy.

>Enny, meany, miney, mo—
>Catch a hormone by the toe,
>Lovely names all meant to soothe;
> the harm of them no one can prove:
>estraderm, estrace; ogen, ovette,
>menrium and micronor; provera and primarin.

Now close your eyes and pick a card.
You do, and get the one that reads
"Pass over heart disease and osteoporosis;
stop at breast cancer."
"Wait!" you say, "I'm in a fix."

"It's okay! Okay?" your doctor
stuffs the deck into a drawer
and orders up a mammogram,
then reassures, "I'll let you choose again next year.
Maybe then you'll get to switch."
Now it's really dark in here.

But, look at it this way,
there's twelve pounds more of you
to scare off buggars in the dark,
and you get a whole new wardrobe—
at Lane Bryant, Ample Woman, and Queen Bee.

You begin to notice men your age
are getting away with murder,
like love handles and thinning hair,
like no annual checkups or D&C's,
like their jokes being flat-out hysterical
to the girl trainers in spandex with big hair
at the fitness center. And you?
Well, tonight you're going to bed with a mystery—
not a man but a book, and you comfort yourself that
somewhere in the world are nice grown people
you brought forth from this tired old body,
and well...you are down from maxi's to mini's:
and at this stage, it's all grateful for small blessings.

And just when you've taken to reading Modern Maturity
and Prevention instead of New Woman and Cosmopolitan,
both of which have not seemed quite as relevant lately,
just when you've finally sneaked a look at 'climacteric'
because you thought all along it meant 'orgasm' and you learn
that it's "the change" and men have one too,
and just when your visits to Merle Norman
are becoming very meaningful (if the raven-haired
nymphette who waits on you will not call you "ma'am"),
and those snippy little twits in black at Dillard's
have become indispensable friends,
and you've exhausted the library's supply of books
with titles like Transitions, Is It Hot in Here? and
150 Questions Mature Women Ask,
and you have a whole shelf of natural remedies including

128

raspberry root bark and cohosh and bioflavonoids,
and just for good measure, Lydia Pinkham Compound
(which is 17% alcohol),
just when you're shored up as much as possible, but still,
all may be possibly lost, and any day now, you could fly
all to pieces and have to be put away
for the rest of your life...like they did Great-aunt Thelma
when she had the Female Hysterics,
just then, and only then,
do you see the light at the end of the tunnel.

It's growing bigger and lighter and wider,
and the best thing of all is, you're moving toward it.
You sit back a little, mop your brow (which is often still wet),
and think about what that sweet daylight might mean:
You are on your way to a coming-out party.
Earrings and mascara and blusher are optional,
ditto Clairol. In the rearview mirror,
there's a certain go-to-hellness tailgating you.
You can see the exit sign and you floorboard it:

      WELCOME TO POST-MENOPAUSAL
         LAND OF THE FREE
         HOME OF THE BRAVE

Isn't that SO? you say, grinning.
Those graffiti girls were right:
Menopause ain't no Tunnel of Love—
Still, a tunnel's a tunnel, not a cave,
and there's light at the far end of it.
And though it's not been the pause that refreshes—
Hell--it's been no pause at all,
you had to work hard the whole time—
still, you're flying out of that tunnel,
you've got zip to lose, and how sweet it is!
You're coming into your powers, whistling Dixie,
full-hearted and full-grown.

You're Bella Abzug, Barbara Jordan,
Germaine Greer and Margaret Thatcher,
with a dash of Susan Powter, Princess Di, and Cher.
You're feeling those wolves running in you.

They're howling and pawing your turf.
You're Lady Wisdom, Moon Woman, Mother Earth.

The Lost Purse Dream
for Rusty

Your eyes light up. You have it too.
Sometimes the one you lose
is cream-colored, cloth.
Mine is almost always black.

We agree we have spent valuable
REM years on fruitless searches.
The last bad night I had with mine
was on a bus in Mexico. I looked
for it among a million chicken cages,
finally called home without it.

We agree we have wasted
our creative subconscious,
that the dream is 100 percent insecurity,
that we should report to our therapists.
Instead, how about,
If I find your purse in my dream,
I'll return it immediately,
no questions asked.

You do the same,
even if it takes a moving van
and an assistant Scheherazade.

Song for Obscure Women

*All these infinitely obscure lives
remain to be recorded.*
      Virginia Woolf
      A Room of One's Own

Yes, Virginia, obscurity recorded:
the lives of women metered out
in a dailiness monumentally unspoken,
a rapture of the objects they tend,
enumeration of the quick, light strokes
of their hands on the baseborn.

Easy enough to say they should
refuse the menial, shun the low;
that the world must change and they,
with it, or by neglect of mention say
these women are not so.

Stand up, my sisters of infinite obscurity,
you who are made noble through the filigrees
and labyrinths of your minds,
the countless renderings of your hands upon reality
which daily overlay the world with a secret order.

We shall record your instances of tenacity,
your stays against insanity
by the sheer mass of your small works—
to right neglect of your shining patience
and say how the earth is saved
by your particulars.

The Pamphlet Lists Ways
to Avoid Being a Victim of Rape

Don't daydream out of doors;
Don't overload your arms;
Don't walk through crowds of men;
Wear a whistle for alarm.

Don't look left or right;
Don't join a crowd for fun;
Don't pause for any reason;
Wear clothes that let you run.

Take as much as several seconds
to analyze and then react
so you do not ride the elevator
with the waiting maniac.

Keep doors and windows locked;
Let no one know you're home:
Put a deadbolt on your door
before you are one.

In conclusion, don't smile,
don't relax, don't play.
Thank you for reading this,
and do have a nice day.

Coign of Vantage

I protest.

"But I am," she says.
And she makes me agree.

Then we name other things
wrinkled:

sand dunes
a newborn's scalp
ripples on a pond
a bloodhound's brow
the chambered nautilus
clouds, and
folds of silk.

Prayers to Skin Goddesses

I. Virgin of Skin Deep

We take your name in vain.
You are indeed deep,
a giant organ, thermostat,
transmitter, integument,
waterproof coat.

You are holding us in;
you are holding them out.
You are our true pajama,
our carry-on luggage.

We haven't another thing to wear.

II. Mother of Pelt

You seek us in the jawline,
a silver wink against the cream.
You bracket us faceside of the ears,
pencil in our upper lips
with heavier smiles.
You oversee our make-overs:

"Brush down lightly," Twenty-two says.

    "Last year it was up."

"I know. But research shows some have it."

    "You mean, don't ruffle our fur?"

"Well...exactly."

Oh Mother of Pelt,
you bring out the beast in us.

III. Our Lady of Surface Illusions

Let it in only a few ways
not be declining.
Favor translucence of brow
glowing like Tiffany glass,
the insides of arms
full of cool silk.

Bless thigh hair for exiting,
the sweat glands for meekness.
Keep liver spots and moles
from games of connect-the-dot.

IV. Pretty-Is-As-Pretty-Does

Help us to make distinctions
between Toning and Masking,
Concentrating and Clarifying,
Energizing and Supporting,
Refining and Hydrating.
May there be pore and pigment
when we have finished.

Cause us to resist such notions
as "coping," "the question of,"
and "problem areas."

When we are too old to prettify,
let us go about calm
in the best and last friend
we'll ever have.

A Woman's Body, Remembering

A hot coin spoke from one side,
a dog of a backache sniped.
The legs were pillars of Samson,
and the head, a swarm of gnats.
Why then, do I miss you,
Aunt Flo, Little Visitor,
Ragtime Sally, Queen's X,
you who have taken yourself away,
tightlipped, silent?

Sometimes I lie in bed calling to you
from the second half of my life.
Remember me?
Remember my useful body?
You came to me, made me
a worker of the world each month,
told me—you comforting clock,
scenic calendar page,
baby maker/trouble maker,
cascade of moon juice,
Rorschach quilt—
that I was all right.

Given one more chance,
I would curl into you for five days,
go sit in my little hut,
without men, without kitchen duty,
curl nights into you,
be an embryo of the moon.

I would begin with ocher clay,
move on to the true flush of poppies,
and finally, would-be baby pink,
all these colors in health—
on a canvas of winning landscape.
This would be folded in linen,
handled only with clean hands,
laid in a cedar trunk,

brought out on feast days
to show my daughters-in-law:
"This is the stuff of your original husband.
Now go and paint your own."

Today, my body remote as an elevated railway,
like soap, like the horizon,
my body wishes to remember.

God's bound to be a woman sometimes,
to think up this bright paint between the legs.
Where else is flowing blood the picture of health,
a lovely joke about the future?

Trip

If I could pull out around this eighteen-wheeler,
impersonate another driver on the Interstate,
maybe in a red Dodge Viper, top down,
leave behind the exhaust of tears,
the second gear of energy that never clicks in—

if I could choose the thoughts of mountains,
set up an easel for a seratonin landscape,
wake to a lookout point, a spectacular view
instead of rats filling my socks; breathe in a valley,
photograph a gorge with the proper distance lens;

if I could flit back through my ancestors,
hit the open road with a jolly grandfather
who brought the sandwiches and a thermos of coffee,
who would allow the radio and gum chewing,
and my arm resting on an open window;

if we could stop every 2 hours at a taffy rest stop,
one with Smokey Mountain tee shirts, genuine
canned Texas air, car deodorizers like baby skunks,
those, and Aunt Parthene's Funnel Cakes, then maybe—
no promises—but just maybe, I could get home.

Believing is Seeing

And these signs shall follow them that believe
Mark 16:17

Eyes that have tracked rabbits, birds, deer
all afternoon across the simple oak
now tear and smart, ready as they are
to discover in the cold Hill Country night
Orion among the hot uncompromising stars.

The astronomer emerges from his lens.
"We have a treat tonight," my son says
and waits until a plane has closed its path.
"First you find Orion by his belt."
His finger points me to the spangled girth.

And then we telescope the Great Hunter:
the yellow-red on his right shoulder named
Betelgeuse, a pulsing variable giant,
and Bellatrix on his left; straight down
find Rigel, making his knee a blue-white glint.

We shiver and our breaths form nebulae
of no order. "The next stars"—my son smiles—
"we'll see together. I have to show you how."
I will to see beyond the late-night books,
the fog of years, the dimming earthly weather.

"Beside the sword you'll see a cloudy mass."
I strain through waves and jerks from here to there,
search Orion's skirt for starry soil.
The cloud mass finally settles to its place.
"You mean the thing that looks like printers' dots?"

"Orion's Nebula," the astronomer says,
then stands against me firm to make a brace.
"Keep looking, Mom. For now, just blink and stare.
I promise you will see them if you try,

and hope—yes, hope for three bright stars."

Minutes go by. The click of the telescope timer
corrects what we cannot—our restless ride
on this galloping star-drenched porch.
And then the gift: three clear and perfect points,
three diamond apples where none were before.

Afraid to blink, I whisper, "Yes, I see them.
Yes." The astronomer's hand tightens on my arm.
"The Trapezium Cluster, at fifteen-hundred light-years."
He laughs. "I give them to you because you see them."
"I take them," I say, and feel him near.

What the Bristlecones Said
for Bob

You take me to see them, bristlecones
you discovered a summer ago.
They hang comic and grand on the edge
of a mile straight down,
Pinus Aristata, endangered species,
a stand or two in six western states.
That's all. At first I wonder what
would be lost, they are so ugly:
gray gnarled trunks suffering from sciatica,
old dogs trying to scratch themselves,
scraggly unsure heads that would have dandruff
if human, and should duck before the blue spruce.
Still, age and oddness due respect,
 we count the rings of one, a section
of trunk sawed down (Only Dead Wood Is Taken,
says the sign for handmade ashtrays)
and estimate it is young—1500 years
give or take a century or two. The odd part—
the trunk is dead: the branches live.
Refusing to come down off their mountaintops,
these stubborn trees make bargain:
they'll look dead, play dead, be sort of dead
in exchange for "home," all the while smiling
in death and birthing little porcupines
glad to snag on anything for a ride
as long as it's traveling higher.
Unbelieving, we touch the branches—
splay of needles with spermy resin
not to leave our hands for hours,
stony arms impervious to rot, cool as mummies.
A mountain bluebird perches atop
one unsaleable pine, July Christmas angel.
In the car, rain dredging the high country,
we eat lunch and puzzle semi-immortality.
We want life dead or alive.
Descending, reviewing the grove
sitting smug as buddha, we ask our god
why he is playing favorites.

On the Way to Cinnamon Pass

Once the mountains staged war,
biting holes in each other.
Now the blood of snows
silvers the gorges
and pines rush down
with a greed of green.
Above the timberline
wildflowers immobilize the world:
scarlet gilia, biscuitroot,
harebell, columbine
weightier than mudslide or snowmass.

What shall we do with this truth?
The deserted mine shafts cry
that if we have a dream,
try hard,
scramble for the lode
we may yet die one night
full of pneumonia,
staring at the tarpaper.

Flowers gamble on the slopes.
Ferns ooze from the clefts.
Lichens in orange and green
mount the slag heaps.
No amount of feet in the world
can trample these moss campion,
penstemon, purple fringe—
no children enough to whiz
these stones across canyons.

The cabins of '92-ers
join the landscape
like deserted beaver lodges,
golden marmots sunning themselves
at imagined doorsteps.
Everything dances
on the downside wind.

Here is yes among old sorrows,
the bleating of lambs
against the first snows
of September.

Bandelier

*From Bandelier National Indian Monument visitors
ascend the steep canyon wall to arrive an hour later
in the atomic development center Los Alamos.*
                                        travel brochure

I.

Lichens stencil every stone,
inscribe with rusts, sulfurs, olives

the ways of the great caldera: frozen lava,
water-eaten canyons, wind-carved sandstone gods

lonely for worshippers.
The ruined village Tyuonyi circles,

the kivas safe in their secrets,
the caves above stained with old fires

and drawings of the hunt, speculating
the return of the basketmakers

gone, it is said, before Coronado
because they could not harness

the wind and sky, could not call down
the rains.

II.

North in Los Alamos, lichens
record the isotopes, lasers, reactors.

They micrograve a rock beside the courtyard pool
in the Bradbury Science Hall,

take note of the ballistic cases
posed like two species of dolphin

jumping in the rarified air,
one for Nagasaki, the other Hiroshima.

The sign says: "One of the greatest
scientific achievements of all time."

In one wing the machines Jezebel and Maniac
demonstrate fission and acceleration.

In another, a letter writer named Einstein
tells President Roosevelt a substance

called uranium might be powerful enough
to blow up a harbor.

III.

The guide has just shown the guests
the models of the warheads.

As they stand listening to the difference
in A and H bombs, a boy of eight,
youngest of a touring party,
goes pale and nauseated.

He lies down on the courtyard bricks
as quietly as the photostatic print
of the child found on a step in Hiroshima.

IV.

In White Rock, a town of scientists,
there is a nuclear physicist
growing a garden—
corn, squash, beans
after the calculations each day,
and a row of apple and pear trees.

He waters the asparagus each evening,

his I.D. tags still jingling from his collar.

Sometimes he goes with his children
to a lookout point 15 minutes from supper,
stares down a half mile of lichened boulders
to the river following south toward the canyon
of the starved-out basketmakers.

He think of their fission:
the splitting of cliffs;
their project:
earth, sky, and water.
He tells his children
there is no change in energy,
only people, when they find it, or fail to.

V.

The child in the caldera of his mother's lap revives,
ready to walk out into the thin air

past the wall of secret orders,
congratulations to the dedicated physicists.

The physicist is hungry; he calls his children,
descends, checks the water hose before going in.

In Bandelier, the lichens,
without true leaf, stem, or root
comfort the north side of stones.

Dear Thunder

You were a horse. I dream of you anyway,
how you and I as centaur take the Weminuche trails
until I, slung down, rest under jackpine at dusk,
the lurch of your walk in the pulse of my legs,
until you, freed of your soaked blankets,
shiver and wheeze relief.

The trail boss tells your history:

     I run him into a brush corral,
left him three-four days,
snubbed him up to a tree
one day more. Fifth day,
on goes the saddle.

     Wild horses,
they're easier'n
barn colts to train.
Wild horses,
they respect a man.

All day we keep up a friendly quarrel,
I jerking you back from biscuitroot, dandelions.
Those times you win, you eat your fill.
Billie, the white mule, lags with us,
ghost in the underbrush scraping his panniers.

Sometimes it is water. You demand slack rein,
take your time, blow bubbles in the recent snow,
steam rising from your nostrils like a dragon's.

Once, lagging behind, you see the others above
on the quarter-mile switchback,
feel your place in line, take off in a trot

that sends my bones to rhythmic hell and back.
Billie, little coward, scurries rear-guard.

Come morning, I walk a mile for your twelve hundred pounds,
step high through the wet gentians and columbines.

Tonight, years later, I hear your hobbles thumping logs,
see the hump of your mustang nose like a mountain ridge.
Tonight I see the lightning, wait out the interval
before your name. I whisper,

We were Chiron.
We were learned in the uses of herbs,
in soft incantations, in soothing potions.

Thunder me what we were together.
Thunder me strength, old horse god.

For Sheep in Transhumance

For them to know their sheepness,
the way they make joy, wide miles of them,
the hush after the cry "They're coming,"
dust of the mountain pass sifting forward,
muted clappering of bellwethers, drifting bleats,
puffballs of sky echoing this tsunami of sheep
rushing to silken green uplands,
to brush corrals and snowmelts,

For them, in some sheepish way,
to see themselves change the road to sheep,
the sharp-sided draw go wool:
placid brown eunuchs shouldering along,
their bells, with each trot, loud beards;
the ashen ewes protecting their udders
with constant detour of slate beds,
lambs gaiting doubletime at their sides,

For the dogs to know how their dripping tongues
and toothed grins betray their love of work:
yap, rush, pivot, surprise
working the stumblers and nibblers,
the curious and slow;

For the herder sun-wizened, nostrils pinched,
hair woolly with road dirt, his horse a martian—
to understand the music of his chant,

For the flock spilling upward to cedar and spruce,
down to riverbed, for the hooves' trotting,
each marking its place with scent bag,
for the sheep's faint notion that, beyond force,
they would move for the pleasure of it:
cells of a corporate beast, pulse of musk,
tangle of wool and hair, gleam of hoof and horn.

May no lupine or death camas spring on their hungry path,
no larkspur or horsebrush present a salad.

Let not the liver fluke trace them down
nor scrapie or foot rot or blue tongue follow.

Have the wolf and the mountain lion pay calls on each other,
the sudden late snowstorm come another year.

May the herder know the treasure of his long day,
his dogs the blessing of their canine luck,

And make all who have met a sea of sheep
going its way to summer pasture
dream the wonder forevermore
when they count themselves to sleep.

Songs of Mesa Verde

I. Little one

I sing for the cups in the rock
    that fit my hands and feet
I sing for the eyes in the rock
    that take me in and out
I sing for the lizard of many horns
    I catch
and for the lizard of feathers
    I do not catch

I laugh and thank my mother
    for fixing my head flat
thank my father
    for fixing my house warm
thank the trees
    for sweet nuts
and the rock
    for sweet water

I say it is good
    to be hot and to be cold
    to ride the turkey
    to swim my hands in the corn
    to make magic in the arms
    of blue trees

II. Young Woman

Never will I stumble
Never will I fall
The new jar of mine
sits on my head
like the nest of a bird

I am the tree
that never falls down
that holds the nest
the nest of corn
the egg of our lives

III. Builder

In my head is the plan

It begins with the tree
Forgive me tree
I cut you for good use

I lay a tree each way
the wind blows
I lay the stones
in the way of the trees

In my head is the plan

The stones go high as my head
when I make them like fish
with water and earth

The stones rise until they stop
stop when they hear
the crop's song above

In my head is the plan

I make eyes with no-stones
I make a mouth and a tongue
for stepping in and out

We will lie in the stones
when the sun takes his gold
We will lie in the stones
as we lay in our mothers

In my head is the plan

If the place is too great
it will fall down
If the place is too narrow
she and I cannot lie together

In my head is the plan

IV. Old Woman

I have not gone out
from this lip of god
for twenty snows
Tomorrow I will not go

I cannot bear the thorns
the sunfire
the heavy way of walking

Tonight my jars are in place
The young ones in my keep
dream their tomorrow

Soon I am a rat
getting into my own store
out of season

Soon I wrap myself
in death skins
I lie down before the great lip

I sing my own death
with a small mouth.

In the Guest House

there's a gray wolf in one corner,
feet planted in contrived tundra,
peering with light eyes around a chair.
His look is mild bewilderment
decided by the taxidermist. Yet
his smell is his own, the curer
never quite able to flush the wildness
from each hair. His scent fills the air.

And though the eyes are yellow glass,
faked windows on his animal soul,
their angle stalks authentic: slanted up,
drawing the muzzle to a near smile,
the important snout sniffing back at the guest,
who crinkles his own at this murky wolf.

All night they smell each other,
one stopped forever in his tracks,
propelling himself in the nostrils
of the other, who thinks he's traveling on.

Rain Dance

It's like this in Texas:
Get your hopes up

over high, silver-cakey clouds,
finally climb out of the pool

go in rejoicing you made it
before the lightning struck

I say rejoicing 'cause
it's still a judgment of God
here in Texas

get dried off and think
of the irony

of being caught in the pool
when the thunderstorm hits

on the hottest day of the year.
Bring in the crying dog.

Close the windows at the first
nasty splats.

Thank God that breeze
is coming off the storm cloud

and then nothing.

It's you're under
the dress of the biggest mamma

in the circus. It's you're
with Poe in the pit.

It's you're in an iron lung
but too healthy for polio.

The clouds, they move
from east to west,

always just north of you.

The clouds, they fart a little
like a school boy on request.

The sun, it comes back grinning
like a satisfied lecher.

Cicadas wind up so sly
you don't know what it is

that's winding you up crazy,
standing, looking out the back door
at where it's not raining.

Postcard wishing you weren't here

A hundred trillion gals. of water backed up
in this lake and I can't remember tonight
which end the dam is damming. Somebody says
3-4 hundred chipmunks in the area all
trained to eat peanuts. Donkey brays on the
1/2 hr. Fridge and water heater in duet.
Trailside Lodge asks you not to put toilet
paper in the toilet, not to walk your
horse in the septic tank area, not to talk
longer than 3 mins., not to go down the
bank to the water. You may feed the chip-
munks 1 bag 25-cent approved peanuts, fish for
a fee, look at the rental boats, buy
dusty catsup in the Gen. Store.Towels
are changed every third day.

Holding Hands

I think of Louis Braille's right hand,
left in Coupvray when the rest of him
was borne triumphant to the Pantheon.

It was that hand gave the blind
of the world their world,
a past of glorious books to read,
and the code buttons
on the elevator.

Did Louis' left hand not know
what his right was about,
his left so entirely mortal,
the 'hand' of handkerchief
nursing his consumption?

Unable to sustain
the hard right hook,
it was just the wingding,
the go-fer, sinister,
left-over, blind-sided hand.
But it's warm in the grave
with the rest of his bones,

all except the right,
back in Coupvray, being noble.

Flying Home

We swim an air-thin ocean inside the wallow-beast.
We pray our kingdoms come, ourselves to live
when the old leviathan stamps our chests on take-off.

Five miles below, roads excuse themselves
with erector-set bridges over rivers,
gallop alongside trains like B-movie bandits.
From this high, the straighter roads distort,
spike into flagpoles. Swamps become streams,
creeks run to rivers. Trees gather along banks
for baptismal services until the waterways
fuse as giant espalier sunning on earth's wall.

Now the earphones, the hot meals tell us
Jonahs run this whale; drag promises from us
to be reasonable, assure us the pilot's temples
are dabbed that wise gray at the pilot factory,
his blue eyes inserted personally by Santa.

Lowering, we see tidal pools shine
like sliced, wet agates; Padre Island
warms in its lamb's wool of waves.
Inland, the farmwoman plots her quilt:
pattern of range, cotton, orchard.

We study a metal fin waggling, shunting,
rearranging flow for descent, and farther,
the horizon where, for an instant,
we puzzle which side of the curve we belong.
Small mouths tell us to drink up, buckle up.
Hands snap buttons in the creature's forehead.

We are on schedule. We know the ground temperature.
Suddenly a hum creeps from our throats, a timid song.
Who says we love least what we do not understand?

Persons Solid and Magical

Digging for the Truth

Raw squirrels and rabbits were his pay
brought to his porch head down,
skins left home for trade.
Never a week went by he didn't
cut a fishhook from a Choctaw's hand.
"Take a big swig of your firewater,"
he'd say, "but leave a little,"
then fetch his quilting thread and needle
and sterilize his knife.
Folks came from miles around
for Charlie Pittman's touch.
He also sang revivals and pulled teeth
but fishhooks were his specialty.

Some say it was because
he had a birthmark on his neck,
not smooth and pink or red
but white and lumpy like a scar.
When he'd inquired, his mother said
he'd started out a frog in the pond,
but Uncle John, fishing one day
had hooked him right there in the neck,
and commencing to skin,
discovered a boy beneath.

He believed the story until he was ten,
told it to his pals and came to be
the laughing stock of Lick Skillet school.

They say he spent the rest of his life
proving people didn't start out as frogs.
The only way to do this was
become an expert in something
where you could dig around for froggy parts
on pretense you were taking out a hook.

When he'd confirmed that they were men
and sewed them up,

he'd burn the hell and tetanus out of them
by emptying their bootleg hooch.
"That's how it burns your guts too,"
he'd kindly say when they got quiet.

He was making sure his mother wasn't right.

Lothario Washington's Work

Waking, he feels the scar on his forehead
where the bullet went in, knows he will
be *feeling* all day—wood, stone, cloth,
the plastic lace of his mother's placemats,
the slick of his daughter's picture
attached to his bureau mirror
kindly sent by his former wife.
His daughter is somewhere distant,
living in the light. He will feel
the no-thanks presence of Charles,
his sister's boyfriend, slipping
into the kitchen where he sits,
getting a cup of coffee, Charles sure
that his stealth can fool a blind man.

But the real work is not these feelings.
The bullet was sent to free his hands
for the women who need him.
God called him late to his life work.

He has Wanda, though she can't be anything
but part-time, what with a long line
waiting for his Braille readings.
The thing is, women are never afraid of him,
come around just asking for his graces.
Nowadays he keeps his glasses on, love-making,
for once, when his lids got loose,
the woman said the sight of his eyes
gave her a vision—she thought
his eyes were little cloud-swirling earths
as seen from the moon.

Lothario tells strangers he's an administrator,
never mind it's love he's administrating,
tending to every round and deep, dry and wet,
including tears, or the possibility
of complete joy. Helping women,
he feels his birthday, Christmas, and oh
especially the Fourth of July, like when
he was a boy, out of the dark coming
sparklers, Roman candles, shooting stars.

Hill Country Bird Woman
for Ammie Rose

In the comics she was feathered, fierce.
She whooshed down to haul you off.
She had a consort and a cohort.
She sprang from an unholy union
of peacock and pterodactyl.

But our Bird Woman is pink,
carries a white downy crown,
walks black-slippered.
This morning she's descended
to open ground, field glasses set.
She declares an oak tree just ahead
to be a clock. If we're lucky,
we'll see her phoebe at ten-thirty.
Bird Woman lowers her glasses.
Now he's the gone-away bird.

Birds are as natural as oatmeal.
They rattle or fuss or tick.
They perch in her dreams in color,
except for egrets, grackles,
and lamb-eating eagles
consigned to black and white.
In nightmares, birds bang at windows,
are gobbled by rat snakes,
flit off without showing
crucial breast or chin or vent.
She wakes weeping,
says the light was poor,
seeks consolation in the arms
of her snowy-crested mate,
a birder-by-marriage.

Our Lady of Hill Country Birds
will talk to a streak of air,
a shaking bush, a jiggling branch.
Birds are holy secrets she incants
in morning vapors or twilights.
For birds' sakes she will humor

the lazy eye, the weak memory,
the best intention.

But Bird Woman has her principles:

"Nature is not always kind."
"Mockingbirds do indeed mock."
"The bluebird is a difficult feeder."
"Sparrows make such good practice."

And her limits:

"You will see more sparrows
than I would wish for you to see."

"God has not granted me the privilege
of loving the boat-tailed grackle."

"Cardinals are worse about getting
into habits than we are."

"Some birders are prone to see
too many exotic birds."

Bird Woman is climbing to aviary nirvana.
If Bird Woman seeks the big Why,
she's nesting it secret as a hummer's egg.
What she likes is the Is of the bird.

So she's chanting its name like a charm,
willing it out of harm's way,
tagging it with love,
declaring a bird is a letter from God
feather-wrapped and sent airmail.

Not Sky or Robin's Egg

My grandmother would say
to her children, Don't
bother your father.
He's having a blue spell.
And the children tiptoed
to their long bitter chores
careful of him on his porch
propped against the wall
in his bowlegged chair.
He pursed his lips,
stroked his beard
as if it were a pet,
frowned that his sturdy self
kept running off like a rabbit
in the woods on a meatless day.
He stared down his sin
of wanting to die.
He was blue.

Years later, that American Gothic
twosome resting in its hillside grave,
the screen on the monitor
in Neuro-Psych reveals
the left frontal lobe
of patients severely depressed
as an island of blue.
Properly dosed, these islanders
lose their quaint geography,
re-form somewhere in the depths,
surface as stable land mass.

All the while she said the words,
Grandmother dripped seven drops
of blueing in her rinse tub,
watched them spread,
knowing the clear water,
lately, dearly up from the well,
was gone forever.

Aunt-Irene-and-Uncle-George

Their names are a seven-syllable word
always said by the family as one.
He took her back to the cap rock,
the only place in Texas that's neat
on the map—and put her on a hill
beside his Mobil station
and tractor repair shop
because he thought that was what
you did with a wife.

The wind had already roared through his ears
20 years and the river 7 miles over and down
had burned deep wordless quicksands in his eyes.
There wasn't any wheat harvest in his blood—
he was born with greasy fingernails—
so he built his shop and pastured old Studebakers
and Ford pickups out back and down a long gully
and stayed on the land.

Meanwhile, she took the little curly-headed girl
he'd spawned in the war when he was on leave
and had lived all over with until '45,
and the straight-headed little girl that came
because they were so glad the war was over,
and made-do in the two-room stucco house
he built for them.

She went down the road every morning
and nursed her sick mother-in-law
in the old homesteader's house with red shutters
behind the athel row, and stayed on
to cook dinner for the hands during wheat harvest—
fried chicken, squash, fresh snapped beans,
and always gravy and mashed potatoes
(her brother-in-law had a thing for chicken wings,
and she had to watch or he'd cuss in front of the girls
if anybody got his) and for dessert—cherry pie

she picked the cherries for
in Evaline and Claude's wild thicket.

At night, when the kitchen was put away—
and without a crumb if you didn't want roaches—
they lay down and heard the wind making love
to the wires and a car or two making love
to the pavement and the coyotes taking over
the whole moonlit hill for their own.
Sometimes there was a possum or a snake
in the chickens and some nights they forgot
to turn off the windmill,
and the tank would be bleeding down
that clear cold cap rock wonder water
all over the girls' swing set next morning.
Some nights a car'd stop out at the shop
and he'd raise up when she punched him
and they'd wait five minutes for them to go away
before he'd get up and climb in his pants
and half lace up his work boots
and struggle out the door
running his hand through his hair
crossing the dirt yard
straining to see if it was a neighbor
needing some gas for town or just
some crazy kids broke down and scared,
and she'd wait barefoot in the crack of the door,
remembering but not letting herself
how he'd taught her to load and shoot the gun.

So the years were a whole long wind
blowing the buffalo grass
and the wheat and the tails of the cows
grazing toward the river.

And through it all there was a big garden
and good close neighbors
just five miles away

and snowstorms when they said

somebody knocked down the fence
between Amarillo and the north pole

and the men came and paved the yard of the shop
with Orange Crush and Hire's Root Beer caps

and Uncle George worked on anything
that ran up and down the road
for 50 miles around including
all the heavy stuff
they brought in to build the dam

and the telephone company came
and replaced all the glass insulators
on the line with plastic gadgets
and stuffed Aunt-Irene's-and-Uncle-George's
dump with enough aqua insulators
snarled in line to choke
every prairie dog hole in Hemphill County.

But then, all of a sudden,
the girls were through at Blue Ridge School
and had to go over the cap rock
and down to the river 30 miles to school.
She told him she thought
she'd move into town with them—
and besides she'd been lonely for 14 years—
but that didn't seem right to him
to do the wind like that

so he built her a first-class house
closer to the road.

She said okay she'd just put her deep freeze
and all her canning jars and Christmas decorations
in the little stucco one
and live like a lady for a change.

And to keep her even happier
he moved the garden

to a new spot to get ride of the nematodes
and quit going to the shop
in the middle of the night
and started keeping his books on paper
instead of in his head.

So for another ten years
she played the piano for their church
of 34 members
and he took up the offering
and gave the Sunday School report.

Then all of a sudden, the curly-headed one
got married and had four of her own
and the straight-headed one
went to be a missionary in Rhodesia.

And now, even though Aunt Irene
has a standing appointment
and sells vitamin products

And Uncle George knocked down his shop
and swept up all the bottle caps
and built a fine new one
right on the same foundation

And even though they both went
to Rhodesia on a vacation

And even though he's a certified meteorologist
and can say before they go to bed
any given night if the good Lord
is going to try to call them home
that night in a storm
that will scrape that new shop
and the little house and the new house
off the wheat plain
like an International Harvester gone berserk:

Even though all this,

they still lie down at night in their
40-year-long Aunt-Irene-and-Uncle-George name
and listen to that wind making love to them,
telling them who they are, who they are,
saying it so sweet
like all the rest of the world
wishes it had only one long name
and knew what to do with 13 inherited acres
out on the cap rock.

In Praise of Woman Chief

Her Gros Ventre mother speaks:

She was taken from me,
snatched as she gathered wood.
She was too young to know
the ways of men.
I was not to cry,
not to go forth for her.
This was the law.
But it was not my heart.
It was not the world
made for my little one.
I cried all night in silence for her.
I asked she be spared the ways of men,
the death of her innocence.

Her Crow captor speaks:

I could not violate her
though I purposed to.
She did not scream and kick.
She asked to keep my horse.
Whoever keeps my god dog
must be loved.
I taught her to shoot.
She rode with me first
on a raiding party
when she was twelve.
Though I say it strangely,
she became my son.

Her "wives" speak:

We would have done
anything she asked.
She was the magic one of us.
She needed hide-scrapers.
She needed lodge-keepers.
We gathered the persimmon

and the chokeberry for her.
We peeled the thistle stick.
She was our mother moon.
We were her four sister stars.

Her companions speak:

The Blackfoot were many.
We were few.
The white man let us
into his fort.
She alone went out
when they signalled
for parley.
We watched with our fingers
like gates before our eyes.
They attacked her
like a buffalo surround.
She shot one dead.
She made two bloody with arrows.
The others turned tail and ran.
In camp, she loved to strike the post
and tell of these coups!

We could not love her in the darkness
like we did other women.
Her touch might have killed us.
Maybe she was a spirit.
Maybe she was a man
in the hide of a woman.
So we let her dance with us,
sit at our ceremonies,
go in to the sacred places.
She was our Joan-of-the-woods
like the one in the French
trapper's tales.

The Gros Ventre chief speaks:

It was an uncertain treaty.
To us, she was Woman Chief,

queen of the Crows.
How did we know
she had come home to visit?
How did we know she was
the same Little Bird
snatched from us
wood-gathering ages ago?
She should have called out
the name of her grandmother.
She should have said words
the French traders taught us.
She should have said
she was home.

Woe unto us!
We have killed
the breath in our mouths.
We have killed our own mother
returning to her bed.

Hello, Darwin?

She is four, pink, with dark bangs.
He wears Birkenstocks and a thin beard.
They stand before the dinosaur exhibit,
she looping his leg as a pillar.

He is leaning over slightly,
telling her this animal is like Barney,
a "creature." Does she know
what a "creature" is? Can she say
Ty-ran-no-saur-us?

"I know, I know," she says,
stamping one little sandaled foot,
as if he is already a fool, so soon,
as if she hasn't seen a hundred times
the previews of *Jurassic Park*.

The timer clicks. Tyran's eyes light up,
his grin widens. From deep in
his mechanical bowels a roar issues:
he steps forth on one lizard-hipped leg.

As light follows sound, so the child
scales her father, shinnies up him
like a seasoned coconut-gatherer,
clawing handfuls of trouser, shirt.
She goes for his neck, then face,
clamors to *become* his face, to climb
inside his head, hide behind his eyes,
disappear into his soul. Now,

she peers out safe as a capuchin,
safe, before she became *homo erectus*,
safe, before she went to pre-kinder,
thought she had learned the whole world.

Icon

for Don

He waits in the alcove, a station of the cross,
his own, built in a wheelchair.
From time to time we step out,
retrieve his bulletin at his feet,
find the hymn, the Bible passage,
prop these in his lost hands.

This morning he can't say even one word
to his wife, to any of us who greet him,
but he can sing, sing the hymn,
"For all the saints who in their order stood."

The high mass of Parkinson's
framed in the arched side aisle,
they must bring the Elements to him,
dipping the bread in the wine,
touching his lips with Christ's body.

A storm breaks in him, a whirlwind on the brain's horizon
appearing out of nowhere, clouds forming in his eyes.

There was a time this weather startled us,
embarrassed us that it embarrassed him.

Now we are envious,
seeing that the Holy Spirit comes upon him,
that he has moved on beyond us halfway to heaven
through his tears, his singing, his prayers—
past appearances, the dignity of the body,
the world of a man's work—Sunday after Sunday
a white shirt, a tie, a pressed suit,
miracle to everyone but himself.

How the Spirit shines out! How rare and beautiful!
A man brings himself forth out of darkness each day,

bestowing the gift of awe on us circling about him.

We would form a line in the darkened side aisle,
stand with folded hands, kneel before his chair,
receive a blessing from his tired hands,
mute tongue, his dark eyes
speaking the testimony of saints.

Symbolism Somewhere

The 400-pound gorilla
sits on his island
surrounded by a deep moat
in the center of the zoo.
Light sparks briefly
in his flat eyes.
There is something
unfunny about him
after gibbons and mandrills.

An old man from nearby
sings out to him
on approach.
From his rolled-up trousers
he fetches two small onions.
He throws them expertly
across the water
where Joe lets them fall
beside him,
lie there awhile
on matter of principle
before tossing them
in his mouth.

It is a hot day.
The man buttons his coat.
"See you tomorrow, old boy."

Here is a thing
better left said
by small onions and
leathery smiles
of feeder and fed.

The Fire-eater of Reynosa

As if the eight lanes of NAFTA Peterbilts
and tarp-covered melon trucks
and camionetas lined with dusty workers
and sedans of señoras headed for bridal showers
and bone-drenched donkeys pulling toothless men
and gaunt boys hopping lanes with bottles of Coca
wasn't enough death waiting to happen,
in the median, with his girlfriend as assistant,
the fire-eater at the last intersection
on the road to the Monterrey cutoff
makes ready.

His eyes are fiery, like the red he wills
on the signal overhead. (He's picked this place
because the red is longest here.) When the sound is
squealing brakes, downshifts, drifting stops,
he drinks naphtha from the pop bottle she holds,
his cheeks bulging in his hairless face,
grabs the sopped torch from her
and prances forward. Clown-ragged, cockeyed,
scarred, he crosses himself, brandishes his torch,
crosses himself twice more.

This is too much! Loco!
The motorists honk, rev engines, inch forward.
Murder comes easily into their hearts.
Would serve him right—to barbecue!
If he's not dead when the light goes green,
they'll finish off the job. He's torture.

Posed deadly still, he suddenly spews a fountain,
lighting the spray with a flourish of torch.
Then, then all time stops—no one knows how long—
because from his mouth there's fire,
flame, beautiful shafts of curling orange.
He's dragonesque, waggles his head
to demonstrate complete control.
The intersection has no place to go,
to look away. The fire-eater is

everybody's sight, time, existence.

In the second before the light turns faulty yellow
in its rush toward green, the fire-eater,
sated with his meal of fire, bows,
and bows again, then leaps away.
Half-sick with bitter taste, the fiery column
printed on his retinas, a little drunk,
he and his assistant frolic in shouts, waves,
a rain of coins, an applause of honking.

And those who cursed him seconds ago
take off for Monterrey, unknown to themselves
redeemed, shot out of this strangest of cannons,
refreshed by the spectacle of cheated death,
unable to say anything except
"Holy Jesus! What a fool! What a miracle!"

McCully's Sod House
(Aline, Oklahoma)

You are walking toward her leading a horse.
She is faced front, the child beside her in a dress
also facing front. She has managed a white apron
but is holding a chicken. She is bent at the waist.

It is 1897. You have gathered everything you own
for the picture. There are six cows and six horses—
some could be rat-tailed mules. Even now on the right
a helper steps from behind his team
to be photographed by the itinerant photographer.

The house is in the center background.
It is a half-acre of stacked-up buffalo sod grass
ripped from a mile away and hauled in by wagon.
For the roof you have split black-jack logs
and laid over more sod.
                    She has sewn flour sacks
together for a ceiling cover. This retards
the raining down of snakes, dirt, and insects.
A sod plow and a buggy complete the scene.

The life expectancy of a sod house is 12 years.
No one knows why yours lasted 60.
Some say it was the presence
of a large elm on the south.

Maybe it is the way you have chosen
to put your left foot out for the picture.
Maybe it is because she went back
to the soddie to change her apron.

Pearl Bell Pittman
1888-1976

She lies a thousand miles away,
all life-support tubes removed.
She breathes in and out, day after day.
I think of her great pendulous breasts
like warm loaves of bread
on which I rested my head in the back seat
through Arkansas and Tennessee one summer—
now shrivelled, crawling under her arms
like little shamed dogs as she lies there.
I see her thighs, hairless,
one bound in a brace since it snapped
one day as she merely stood:
seven babies came through these posts
(the seventh she told me of
one rainy afternoon sitting in
a certain gray armchair—
I horribly fascinated
over the dead baby's perfect curls,
the prettiness of his face,
Grandfather wrapping him up
and taking him out back.)

Her hands twist open jars of pickles,
tomatoes, okra, black-eyed peas;
they skin onions, pluck feathers
from steaming headless chickens,
flick pinches of baking powder into biscuit dough.
They pick about in the turnip greens
for her favorite piece of hog jowl.
Delicate now, the tough stiff fingers
lift the canaries' cage door,
set in the lid of crumbled egg yolk.
She has me come to see the two eggs
in the corner nest, "quietly so as not

to disturb the motherbird."

I see her great astounding Victorian body—
six-foot-tall bride with a sober hand
resting on Grandfather's sitting-down shoulder.
The wedding—a Sunday night after revival meeting,
a trip three miles in a buggy home to her house,
a sister going upstairs with her
to help with a white nightgown,
wide pink satin ribbon woven down the front,
how she trembled when her sister left her
at the top of the stairs,
how she righted herself with a small smile
when Grandpa, ascending, said,
"Why Pearl, you look so pretty!"
(She wouldn't tell me more.
He had been dead fifteen years
that afternoon.)

I think of her as a seven-year-old
on a train three days and nights
from Mississippi to Texas,
women and children in the passenger car,
men two cars back with the cattle
and household goods.

Another trip later, much later,
her first-born dying in her arms
for want of milk. She rode two
summer days in a wagon to exchange
David Lee for his cousin.
Home again with a strange baby,
fat and ready for weaning to the cup.

Now my Amazon grandmother
lies a great broken continent,
a land over-grazed:

breast tumor removed, colon unobstructed,
cataracts frozen, skin cancers erased,
bladder dilated—all the unnecessary,
acting-up parts long since removed—
womb, tonsils, appendix, gall bladder.

I want to get in bed beside her,
warm myself against her massiveness,
hear the punctuating sucks and clicks
her tongue makes cleaning her teeth
of chicken bits as she thinks of the next part
to the story she is telling.

I want to line up like a paper doll with her,
staring straight ahead on a genealogy chart—
my mother between us holding our hands.

I want to pick through the homestead
in the Indian Territory
for corset stays, sachet bags,
her churn lid, next year's dahlia bulbs.
I want to tell her it is all right
to have lived thinking mainly about
turnips and egg custard, the neighbor's child
with polio, whether the road out front
will be oiled down today or tomorrow.

A part of me lies in her eighty-eight-year-old
death-ridden body.
A part of her walks in the form I still bear.

Goodnight, my Amazon lady.
Thank you for my bones.

South by Southwest

In the High Desert

It is the yearning hour,
when gold touches the mesas.
Something there is
that may not love these buttes,
but we don't care to know it.
Here's a parade of the eons,
an interruption of sky,
a party of giantesses dressing:
Shall their aprons be red?
Their blouses cream? ochre?
Perhaps mauve skirts?
They have already placed
their jewels of trees.
Posing as temples, moonscapes,
they hold the secret of fractals,
know all life below as diminutive.
They fling down striations,
god-thoughts, and silence.

The Roma Bluffs: Still Life with Folk

But why should love stop at the border?
Pablo Casals

Sunday afternoon, high above the Rio Grande,
we stand on a promontory rare for this delta.
Here riverboats delivered sugar, flour, salt,
returned the venturing settlers to Brownsville.
Today, the river is the only safe swimmer,
lips sealed to the media's descriptions:
drug, secure, international, illegal.

Across, a picnic family poses against mesquite.
A man tends the fire; others skim rocks.
Women chat, balance babies on hips.
Kids refuse the still life—shout, throw mud.
From the thin woods, like a cunning stray dog,
a huge sow meanders, her five piglets trailing.
The women scream, then laugh, swoop up
their toddlers hard bent on new piglet toys.

Upstream, the father of water-gatherers
has backed his pickup down an old boat landing
where five-gallon buckets form a pallet:
viridian, Dutch pink, cadmium yellow, cream.
The tallest boy, braced waist-high in the eddies,
dips what's escaped Juarez, Big Bend, Laredo,
hands it to his brothers and cousins.

From the little town on the low horizon
drifts faint accordion, *guitarrón, vihuela,*
announcement of a *futbol* game and *lotería.*

Brueghel the Elder would be thrilled:
gray Gulf clouds, light green of woods,
a distant bridge, Sunday calm.

Not *l'art pour l'art,* still, here's a tableau
the art lover could pause over, arms crossed,

eyes resting from modernity. This canvas
could be auctioned at Southby's, be precious,
collected, in its genre Rockwellian way.

While the church bell in Miguel Aleman clangs
evening vespers, the surveillance camera
high above us moves robotic, irregular, cunning.
Somewhere we appear on a screen
waving back to the Mexican children as we go.

We will carry this scene behind our eyes
and in coming days suppose families
doing things families do at river's edge:
drawing water, eating, communing.
We wish them repose. Perhaps,
there will even be harmony, perspective,
light and shade. For now, the old question
of knowing: If a landscape is out of sight...?

Take a good look, we tell ourselves, and send
the same advice across the inscrutable water.
Life may imitate art, but upstream, downstream,
or across, the Great Border Wall of the Rio Grande
will overpaint this riverscape forever.

Proof

Two miles north of the border
in a canal, he was found
halfway under water.

The fact: he wasn't dead
from the shotgun blast
to the back of his head.

Several inches wide,
said the sheriff,
and twenty hours old,
according to what
the man told:
that the sun was
going down
when they drove him
out from town.

He actually talked,
told the time
and his name,
admitted he had
just crossed.

They couldn't charge him
as an overstay,
or detainee.
Oh, he was wet all right,
but still, documented:
"Man Thought Dead
Is Actually Alive"
so the headline read.

The Golden Rain Tree

Around Columbus Day a constellation descends,
covers lawns in the Valley with millions of yellow stars
like the cool light film of a solar eclipse.

Maybe these trees begin their reign as wood deities.
Maybe they rain their version of "cats and dogs."
For sure, they are not reining themselves in.

Days later delicate pill boxes appear with seeds
that soon enough medicate our grass and flower beds.
Some declare the golden rain tree a noxious invasive.

We know this but we have other labels.
While northerners revel in the color show of forests
and children stick oak cut-outs to classroom windows,

winter crops line our roadways with electric green.
In the Australia of Texas, we need some assurance
that the earth is indeed tilting on its axis.

We look to the golden rain tree, its clustering pods,
first golden, then pink, turning orange, oranger, orangest.
Here is our seasonal salvation, eye candy for autumn.

The Valley of Flocks

I.
Green parakeets shriek
bird delirium overhead,
dissolve into a hackberry,
chitter the husks from seeds,
jet off in screech-fest.

II.
The *Virgen* appears
on curtains, Camaros, trees.
She assembles her faithful,
gathers them unto herself,
queen of the sweetest of crowds.

III.
At Pepe's on the River,
no more bottles of beer on the wall
or anywhere else, a winter afternoon
when a swarm of Snowbirds quaffed
198 pitchers of *la buena vida.*

Cicadas

They wake you at dawn—
white noise, static,
high blood pressure,
gears without oil.

They sizzle the sun up
like New Caledonian
wizards danced it up,
call out the nerves
like militia, proclaim
the day'll be fried.

They pull a dance card
making irritation
all the rage,
"frazzled" a fatal verb,
"incessant" a catch word,
"crazy" your mantra.

They've waited
17 years underground
for this moment,
determined to be
your preferred
sound system.

Medley of a Mockingbird on a Rainy Dawn

I don't have to carry water
in my mouth to my fledglings—
Glory Hallelujah! as the humans say.

My birdies are about to drown
because I made their nest too tight.
Can't win for losing!

This stuff streaking past me in the trees—
do I sing to it too?

I promise I have sung the hours of the night,
like a monk on duty.

Finally, my color—gray!

Come, come and love me anyway, nearby mate.

I am mockingbird; therefore, I am.

I don't know a spring shower from a hurricane.
It's best this way.

I'm all alone in this worldwide job;
what's the holdup, sun?

The War on Grackles

Our mayor says we must make war on grackles
as well as any that are in company with them,
like starlings, cowbirds, crows—in a word,
all dark birds who gather for evening vespers
on wire and trees at Luby's and Max's making
unamused diners and readers run to their cars,
heads covered by the evening news.

But the wires hum like running sixteenth notes,
like messages, finally, from outer space,
the twittering of bird cocktail hour dissolving
into sizzling raucous gossip and ending in
screeching hurrahs just as the black evening
fingers them from the east, trumping their blackness.
(Starlings are ready, with their chests full of stars.)

The city commission has set field strategies:
firecrackers, power hoses, alarm horns,
plastic snakes and owls, electrified doggie wire.
After the wars on drugs, cancer, and terrorists,
we need war on birds? War spelled backwards is raw:
as in exposed, fleshy, uncooked; also unadorned,
open, original—like black birds on wires.

Geophone Thumpers

They tell us to remain calm,
stop writing letters to the editor;
only a few more weeks
of this all-night thumping,
giant vibrators roaming the streets
of our borderland,
plumbing for oil or gas beneath us.

Our dreams are filled with jumbo rabbits
scratching themselves at leisure
beneath our front flower beds,
with hobbits doing the naughty
on the undersides of our trade-zone roads,
the Border Patrol on alert.

The really frightening dream, though,
is when, after the vibrations
have reached three miles down,
and where our kids and the neighbors'
have been digging a hole all summer
for a swimming pool,
China pokes its head through.

Drought

Some days we're only tied to heaven
by the word named "rain,"
small heavy sound intoned
as all the proof we have of hope.

In a saddened land,
where birds fill us with obligation
waiting beside their clay bowl,
we take any fluff of sky,
however white and promiseless,
vow to love its fingering shadow
passing over us, the only thing
between us and a dry god.

Road *Ropa*

Explain the baby's bootie on the center stripe,
the red tie crossing the road like a snake.
A wet boy shivers home without his towel;
a girl hunts for her Tuesday panties,
a child wears only a pajama top.
Workers limp about in right or left boots,
night ladies in a lone silver pump.
There are socks enough in the streets
to hang on all hearths at Christmas.
A schoolboy misses his track shoes.

Every piece of road *ropa* has its own story,
its *cuento* of laughter or woe, its extremis.
How it got there is hardly neutral:
flung in fits of anger, revenge exacted,
or abandoned in ecstasy,
with a few jiggled, slid, or bumped.
(You, wind, are opportunist supreme.)

Books and lighters and bills,
ID's, schedules, sunglasses,
knives, screwdrivers, bolts—
knowing that things in their rightful places,
rightly used, are a bore—
these dragsters and streetwalkers,
homecoming parades
for the School of the Disturbed,
homeless veterans of domestic wars
all waving, sighing, cheering,
call out "Help and Hello!
Anybody! Put and pull us on,
reunite us with our twins, use us!
Please, into your pockets, your purses!
Make us fall in love again!
Above all, get us off the streets!"

Eating Texas

It's taken a long apprenticeship
to make waffles in the shape of Texas.
First there were mountains over Waco.
Then the Panhandle sank.

A few more false starts when
the Red River swamped Oklahoma
and the Rio Grande dripped into Mexico.
Now I can make perfect ones.

All I have to do is take care
to stop pouring the batter a little shy
of El Paso, Dalhart, and Texarkana.
For some reason, Brownsville needs more.

Otherwise, my grandchildren complain they
don't have the tail of Texas to bite off.